TIME FOR SEX

45% of married couples, 61 33% of lesbians and 67% of gay men who have been together up to two years have sex at least three times a week.

TIME FOR MONEY

If the Indians who sold Manhattan Island for $24 in 1624 had put that money in a bank at 8% compounded interest, it would be worth $52 trillion today.

TIME FOR SCHOOL

American teenagers spend an average of 38 hours per week in class or studying. Japanese teenagers spend 59 hours.

TIME FOR MARRIAGE

The average American marriage lasts 9.4 years.

TIME FOR READING

44% of Americans do not read a single book in a year—which means they will miss out on the #1 book of the year for "Jeopardy" fans, trivia buffs, and curiosity seekers—

IT'S ABOUT TIME!

Hundreds of Fascinating Facts About How We Spend It, Fill It, Buy It, and Defy It

---

ROBERT L. SHOOK is the author of more than 30 nonfiction books. His son and coauthor, MICHAEL J. SHOOK, is a student at Colorado State University. Their previous collaborations include *The Book of Odds* (Plume).

IT'S ABOUT TIME!

Michael D. Shook
and Robert L. Shook

A PLUME BOOK

PLUME
Published by the Penguin Group
Penguin Books USA Inc., 375 Hudson Street,
New York, New York 10014, U.S.A.
Penguin Books Ltd, 27 Wrights Lane, London W8 5TZ, England
Penguin Books Australia Ltd, Ringwood, Victoria, Australia
Penguin Books Canada Ltd, 10 Alcorn Avenue,
Toronto, Ontario, Canada M4V 3B2
Penguin Books (N.Z.) Ltd, 182–190 Wairau Road, Auckland 10, New Zealand

Penguin Books Ltd, Registered Offices: Harmondsworth, Middlesex, England

First published by Plume, an imprint of New American Library,
a division of Penguin Books USA Inc.

First Printing, October, 1992
10 9 8 7 6 5 4 3 2 1

LIBRARY OF CONGRESS CATALOGING-IN-PUBLICATION DATA:

Shook, Michael D.
It's about time! / Michael D. Shook and Robert L. Shook.
p. cm.
ISBN 0-452-26852-4
1. Handbooks, vade-mecums, etc. 2. Time—Miscellanea. I. Shook, Robert L. 1938– II. Title.
AG105.S545 1992
031.02—dc20 92-53553
CIP

Printed in the United States of America
Set in Garamond Light
Designed by Eve L. Kirch

This book is for Sarah
—MDS

CONTENTS

ACKNOWLEDGMENTS

We are grateful to the following people who helped us in writing this book: Ari Deshe, Ann Geupel, David Goldman, Kara Gutterman, Gregory Holtz, Cory Hubbert, Tammy Kaplan, Brett Leukart, Jeff Meyer, Jon Meyer, Matt Meyer, Mark Mitchell, Dan Rinehart, Ann Roskem, Will Roth, Carrie Shook, Elinor Shook, RJ Shook, Rod Simpson, Tom Sloan, Eddie Stern, Robert Stern, Danny Thomases, Jenny Traeger, and Ed Ziv. Special acknowledgment goes to Mary Liff, whose typing and organizational skills saved us a tremendous amount of time (remember, "It's About Time"). And we appreciate Jeff Herman, our agent, and Ed Stackler, our editor, both of whom are exceptional in their areas of expertise. As a team, we had a grand time writing this book; we hope the reader has a wonderful time reading it.

INTRODUCTION

A book's introduction has an obvious mission, which is to introduce what the author(s) has written to the reader.

It's about time.

Yes, and it's about time somebody wrote this book. In it, you will learn a lot about time that you always wanted to know. And you'll find things that you never thought about before but will enjoy learning. After all, when it comes to time, it's a subject in which we all have a vested interest. Each of us has a finite amount of time—so we should make the best use of it while we can. For instance, of the 1,440 minutes in each 24-hour period, the average American between the ages of 18 and 64 spends 28 minutes dressing, and 26 minutes going to and from work. He or she devotes about 7 minutes to religion. As writers who spend many hours each day pounding away at our word processors, we, in particular, find it somewhat annoying that the average American between 18 and 24 spends only 5 minutes a day writing! And, 44 percent of American adults do not read a single book during the course of a year (we don't like this statistic either).

Speaking of doing a lot of things on a busy day, on May 25, 1935, in a track meet in Ann Arbor, Michigan, Ohio State track star Jesse Owens set or matched six world records in a period of 45 minutes! Like Jesse, a lot of Americans like to do things fast—this is probably why 20 percent of us will eat at a fast-food restaurant today—1 in 20 will eat at a McDonald's.

Let's slow things up a bit . . . Did you know that your hair grows an average of about an inch every 8 weeks? Your fingernails and toenails are much slower, growing at the pace of an inch in about 4 years. It takes about 6 months to build a single Rolls-Royce, whereas only 13 man-hours are exerted to assemble a Toyota car. And every 17 minutes, another franchise opens in the United States . . . It's a good thing too—in mid-1990, the world's human population was 5.3 billion, and is increasing by 145 million newborns each year. That's 395,000 a day, which is a lot of mouths to be fed. And what will our planet be like in the future? Each year, 27 million acres of tropical rain forests are destroyed—an area equal in size to the state of Ohio!

For anyone who is curious about how long things last, here are a few facts that will surprise you: The average American marriage lasts 9.4 years. Women's extramarital affairs last, on average, 21 months, whereas men's go on for 29 months. And to really switch gears, a Boeing 747 is designed to fly 60,000 hours, and undergo 210,000 takeoff and landing cycles in a period of 20 years.

There's much more we can tell you about *It's About Time!* but right now, we're just introducing it. But what we can tell you is that there is something for everybody, ranging from sex to money (two very popular subjects). For instance, happily married couples have sex 75 times a year. Now about money—when the Indians sold the island of Manhattan to the Dutch in 1624, a transaction for which they received $24, they really didn't get such a bad deal—their mistake was that they should have invested their money more wisely. Had the Indians put it in a Dutch bank and collected compound interest at an annual rate of 8 percent, by 1993, their money would have been worth $52 trillion—more than the total present value of all the property located on Manhattan! If you have the inclination, there is much more interesting and practical information about compound interest.

Be sure to give yourself plenty of time to read *It's About Time!* Because when you do, you won't be able to put it down—you're going to have the time of your life.

MDS and RLS

I. How We Spend Our Time

Traveling to/from Work

The average American between ages 18 and 64 spends 26 minutes per day traveling to and from work.

SOURCE: AMERICANS' USE OF TIME PROJECT, UNIVERSITY OF MARYLAND, 1985.

Traveling to the Store

The average American between ages 18 and 64 spends an average of 19 minutes per day traveling to and from stores.

SOURCE: IBID.

Time Sleeping

The average American between ages 18 and 64 sleeps an average of 7.7 hours a night. Americans age 64 and older sleep a little more, averaging 7.9 hours a night and 34 minutes of napping each day.

SOURCE: IBID.

Dressing Takes Time

The average American between ages 18 and 64 spends 28 minutes a day dressing.

SOURCE: IBID.

Time at Parties and Bars

The average American between ages 18 and 64 spends about an hour and a half per week at parties and bars. SOURCE: IBID.

Travel for Social Activities

The average American between ages 18 and 24 spends 16 minutes per day traveling to and from social activities.

SOURCE: IBID.

It's Mealtime!

The average American spends 6 years of his or her life eating, or 8 years if he or she goes to restaurants a lot.

SOURCE: DAN DANBOM, *AMERICAN DEMOGRAPHICS*, MAY 1990.

Talkative Waiters

Americans who dine out spend 8 months during their lives listening to the list of daily specials. SOURCE: IBID.

Returning Calls

The average American spends 2 years during his or her lifetime returning telephone calls. There is only a 17 percent chance of reaching a businessperson on the first call.

SOURCE: IBID.

Where Are My Glasses?

During the average American's life, a year is spent looking for misplaced objects. SOURCE: IBID.

Opening Mail

The average American spends 8 months of his or her life opening mail. SOURCE: IBID.

Visiting Friends

Americans age 18 to 64 spend about 5 hours a week visiting friends or relatives. Americans 65 and older spend 3.85 hours a week visiting people.

SOURCE: AMERICANS' USE OF TIME PROJECT, UNIVERSITY OF MARYLAND, 1985.

Time Spent Talking

Americans age 18 to 64 spend about 4.3 hours per week talking. Women average 5.1 hours per week, whereas men average 3.5 hours per week. SOURCE: IBID.

Gone Shopping

Married females spend an average of 7.2 hours per week shopping, and married men shop 4.9 hours per week. Unmarried females spend an average of 6.3 hours shopping, whereas unmarried men shop 4.3 hours a week. Females with postdoctorate education shop an average of 8.4 hours per week. Males with postdoctorate education shop 3.8 hours per week.

SOURCE: *AMERICAN DEMOGRAPHICS*, FEBRUARY 1989.

Classified Shopping

In a typical month 41 percent of females and 49 percent of males have looked through the classifieds.

SOURCE: *ROPER REPORTS*, JULY 1989.

Too Much TV

Female teens watch TV an average of 21 hours, 18 minutes per week. Male teens average 22 hours, 36 minutes. Females age 18 to 34 watch an average of 28 hours, 53 minutes, and males this age watch 25 hours, 44 minutes. Females age 35 to 54 watch an average of 32 hours, 28 minutes, and males this age watch about 27 hours. Females age 55 and over watch about

41 hours of TV each week, and males in this category watch 37 hours, 32 minutes.

SOURCE: *1990 INFORMATION PLEASE ALMANAC*. HOUGHTON MIFFLIN.

Grooming

Females between ages 18 and 24 spend 7.5 hours a week grooming. Males this age spend 5.3 hours a week on grooming.

SOURCE: *AMERICAN DEMOGRAPHICS*, NOVEMBER 1989.

Teeth Cleaning

In the last 24 hours: 22 percent of females brushed their teeth more than twice and 18 percent of males; 30 percent of females and 20 percent of males have flossed their teeth; 43 percent of females and 37 percent of males have used mouthwash.

SOURCE: *ROPER REPORTS*, MAY 1989.

Time Spent Studying

American teenagers spend an average of 38 hours per week in class or studying. Japanese teenagers spend 59 hours and Soviet teenagers spend 51.5 hours.

SOURCE: *THE NEW YORK TIMES, NEWSWEEK.*

Tying a Necktie

The average American male spends 4 hours a year tying his necktie!

SOURCE: 1991 *INFORMATION PLEASE ALMANAC*. HOUGHTON MIFFLIN.

Child Care

Mothers with 1 or more children age 5 or over spend an average of 6 hours a week on child care. Fathers average 2 hours per week. Mothers with 1 or more children under age 5 spend an average of 17 hours a week on child care. Fathers average 5 hours per week. Mothers who have only a grade-school education spend approximately 6 hours a week, whereas fathers with only a grade-school education spend 2 hours per week. Mothers who are college graduates average 12 hours a week taking care of their children, whereas fathers who graduated spend 5 hours a week on child care.

SOURCE: *AMERICAN DEMOGRAPHICS*, JULY 1989.

Time Spent Eating

Females age 18 to 24 spend 6.6 hours per week eating. Males this age spend 7.2 hours per week.

Females age 35 to 44 spend 7.8 hours per week eating. Males this age spend 7.7 hours per week.

Females age 55 to 64 spend 9.9 hours per week eating, while men this age spend 10.7 hours.

Employed females spend 7.1 hours per week eating, while unemployed females spend 9.2 hours a week eating.

Employed men spend 7.8 hours a week eating, while unemployed men spend 9.8 hours a week eating.

SOURCE: *AMERICAN DEMOGRAPHICS*, NOVEMBER 1989.

Preparing Meals

On an average day females spend 51 minutes preparing meals, whereas men spend 15 minutes.

SOURCE: TOM HEYMANN. *ON AN AVERAGE DAY*. FAWCETT, 1989.

Time Out for Reading

Americans between the ages of 18 and 64 spend about 2.8 hours per week reading books, newspapers, and magazines. This figure jumps to 4.1 hours a week for college graduates and 4.4 hours per week for people who attended graduate school. Americans between the ages of 18 and 24 read 1.6 hours a week compared with 4.5 hours per week for people between ages 55 and 64. The figure jumps to almost 6 hours for Americans over 65.

SOURCE: AMERICANS' USE OF TIME PROJECT, UNIVERSITY OF MARYLAND, 1985.

Reading Time

The average adult American reads just 24 minutes a day. This is down by about 25 percent since 1965. Roughly half of American adults never read books or magazines.

SOURCE: STRATFORD P. SHERMAN, "AMERICA WON'T WIN TILL IT READS MORE," *FORTUNE*, NOVEMBER 18, 1991, P. 201.

More Free Time

The average male retiree has 25 free hours a week, whereas females average 18 hours per week.

SOURCE: AMERICANS' USE OF TIME PROJECT, UNIVERSITY OF MARYLAND, 1985.

Takes Time to Pay for Taxes

The average American spends 4 months a year or about one-third of his or her adult life working for the government.

SOURCE: DAN DANBOM, *AMERICAN DEMOGRAPHICS*, MAY 1990.

Waiting in Line

The average American spends 5 years waiting in line.

SOURCE: IBID.

Outdoor Sports

Americans between the ages of 18 and 64 spend an average of 2.2 hours per week playing outdoor sports—2.9 hours for men and 1.5 hours for women.

SOURCE: AMERICANS' USE OF TIME PROJECT, UNIVERSITY OF MARYLAND, 1985.

Time Spent on Religion

The average American between the ages of 18 and 64 devotes approximately 48 minutes per week to religion—1 hour for females and 36 minutes for males. The average jumps to 1.75 hours for Americans over age 65. SOURCE: IBID.

Listening to Music

The average American between the ages of 18 and 64 spends 18 minutes a week listening to music. Americans age 65 and over spend 49 minutes a week listening to music. SOURCE: IBID.

Kids Earn TV Degrees

The average kindergarten student has seen more than 5,000 hours of TV, having spent more time in front of the TV than it takes to earn a bachelor's degree.

SOURCE: U.S. DEPARTMENT OF EDUCATION.

Car Phones

The average monthly cellular phone bill for the 4.4 million car phones in the United States for the first 6 months of 1990 was $89.30. The average length of calls was 2.3 minutes.

SOURCE: CELLULAR TELECOMMUNICATIONS INDUSTRY ASSOCIATION.

Volunteer Work

In 1989, 98 million Americans did some volunteer work. On average, volunteers devote 4 hours per week. In 1989, the 10.5 billion hours of service rendered were valued at $170 billion.

SOURCE: 1990 GALLUP ORGANIZATION STUDY.

Summer Vacations

The average duration of overnight summer vacations in 1991 was about 4.9 nights; 6 percent go on day trips, 10 percent go for 1 night, 41 percent go for 2 or 3 nights, 33 percent go for 4 to 9 nights, and 10 percent go for 10 or more nights.

SOURCE: U.S. TRAVEL DATA CENTER.

Computer Use

Americans between the ages of 18 and 64 spend an average of 21 minutes a week on the computer compared with Americans over age 64 who spend 98 minutes per week on the computer.

SOURCE: AMERICANS' USE OF TIME PROJECT, UNIVERSITY OF MARYLAND, 1985.

Time Spent Writing

The average American age 18 to 24 spends just 5 minutes a day writing.

SOURCE: IBID.

The Work Week

Here is diary record of the average number of hours a week spent at paid work, including the commute to work, by men and women employed 10 or more hours a week (1985).

AGE	MEN	WOMEN
18 to 24	36	34
25 to 34	44	31
35 to 44	43	32
45 to 54	46	32
55 to 64	36	29
65 and older	30	22

EDUCATION	MEN	WOMEN
Grade school	45	29
Some high school	45	33
High-school graduate	42	32
Some college	42	30
College graduate	40	32
Postgraduate	38	34

HOUSEHOLD INCOME	MEN	WOMEN
Under $15,000	37	31
$15,000–$24,999	41	32
$25,000–$34,999	42	30
$35,000 and over	41	32

MARITAL STATUS	MEN	WOMEN
Married	42	30
Unmarried	41	33

NUMBER OF CHILDREN	MEN	WOMEN
None	42	32
One or more age 5 or older	40	32
One or more under age 5	45	24

DAY	MEN	WOMEN
Monday	7	5
Tuesday	8	6
Wednesday	8	6
Thursday	7	6
Friday	7	5
Saturday	3	2
Sunday	2	1

SOURCE: IBID.

Outdoor Chores

Men spend 1.4 hours per week doing outdoor chores compared with women, who spend about a half hour doing outdoor chores. SOURCE: IBID.

Home Repairs

Men spend 1.8 hours per week doing home repairs compared with women, who spend .4 hours a week doing home repairs.

SOURCE: IBID.

Housework

The average man spends .3 hours per week doing laundry or ironing, whereas women average 2.2 hours doing these chores. Men spend 1.4 hours per week housecleaning compared with women, who spend 5.1 hours a week doing housecleaning.

SOURCE: IBID.

Meal Cleanup

Men spend .4 hours a week cleaning up after meals, whereas women spend 1.9 hours per week. SOURCE: IBID.

Taking Care of Children

In 1985 mothers spent 9 hours a week doing primary child-care activities, compared with 7 hours in 1975 and 8 hours in 1965. Fathers spent 3 hours per week on primary child care. The figure jumped to 17 hours per week for mothers of pre-schoolers and 6 hours by fathers. SOURCE: IBID.

On the Road

Men spend approximately 11 hours per week traveling, whereas women spend about 9 hours. SOURCE: IBID.

Mowing the Lawn

The average lawn, which is about 6,000 square feet, takes about an hour to mow. With a 21-inch push mower someone walking slowly at 1.7 mph will take about 3½ hours to mow an acre; someone walking faster at nearly 3 mph will take about 2 hours. A rear-engine riding mower will mow an acre in about 1 hour; a front-engine riding mower will mow it in about 45 minutes to 1 hour. A lawn and garden tractor will mow an acre in about 30 to 45 minutes, and a 60-inch mower deck will mow an acre in about 30 minutes. An estimated 100 million Americans spend nearly 1 billion hours a year operating 61 million mowers to tend a lawn the size of Indiana (about 25 million acres or 39,000 square miles).

SOURCE: JOHN DEERE.

Schick's Shtick

The average American male spends about 3,500 hours shaving during his lifetime. Based on an 8-hour workday, that averages 437½ days, or 1 year and 2½ months! However, it's time well spent. If left untended, the average beard would grow to 27.5 feet.

SOURCE: SCHICK RAZOR COMPANY.

Weekend Work

The average American spends the following time doing these activities on weekends:

Cooking	2 hours
Working at home	2 hours, 54 minutes
Making household repairs	1 hour, 12 minutes
Running errands	1 hour, 43 minutes
Grocery shopping	59 minutes
Cleaning	2 hours, 17 minutes
Laundry	1 hour, 18 minutes
Paying bills	34 minutes

SOURCE: HILTON WEEKEND LEISURE TIME SURVEY OF 1,000 ADULTS.

Make Every Minute Count

Based on a life expectancy of 72 years, anything you do that takes 20 minutes a day, over a lifetime, equals 1 year. Think about this when you drive to work every day, talk on the telephone, wait in lines, watch TV, and so on.

SOURCE: AUTHORS' CALCULATIONS.

Frequent Shoppers

Men, not women, shop more frequently. And young people shop more than older people. A 1991 survey revealed that 10.8 percent of men shop every day while 7 percent of women do. 11 percent of Americans under the age of 45 shop every day, compared with 6 percent of those 45 and older. It is probable, however, that men do more fill-in shopping, whereas women shop in more extensive, less frequent trips. 9 percent of the entire U.S. population shopped every day during 1991.

SOURCE: MARITZ MARKETING RESEARCH INC.

Waiting Time for a New York Taxi

The average waiting time for a taxi in New York City is less than 5 minutes.

SOURCE: YELLOW CABS OF NEW YORK.

How People Spend Their Time on New Year's Eve

A 1989 poll revealed that Americans spend New Year's Eve in the following ways:

Celebrate quietly with friends	45%
Go to party or club	25%
Don't celebrate	28%
Other	9%

SOURCE: THE ROPER ORGANIZATION

Spending Time by the Fireplace

In a survey made for Duraflame, here are the favorite activities of Americans in front of their fireplaces:

Being romantic	29%
Visit with family and/or friends	25%
Watch television	13%
Read a book	12%
Listen to music	9%
Other	12%

SOURCE: R. H. BRUSKIN ASSOCIATES

2. The First Time

The First Olympic Games

The first recorded Olympic Games were held in 776 B.C., and consisted of one event, a great footrace of about 200 yards. The modern Olympic Games started in Athens in 1896.

SOURCE: *1991 INFORMATION PLEASE ALMANAC*. HOUGHTON MIFFLIN.

Early Start

The average age at which a federal prisoner first fired a gun is 13.2 years old. SOURCE: U.S. DEPARTMENT OF JUSTICE.

6 Records in 45 Minutes

On May 25, 1935, Jesse Owens equaled the 100-yard record of 9.4 seconds while running for Ohio State University in the 35th annual Western Conference meet held in Ann Arbor, Michigan. Ten minutes later he jumped an incredible 26 feet, 8¼ inches, a world record for the broad jump. Twenty minutes later, in the 220-yard sprint, he not only established a new world record of 20.3 seconds, but also simultaneously beat the 200-meter record. A quarter of an hour later he set a new world record of 22.6 seconds, for the 220-yard low hurdles and at the same time broke the 200-meter record. In 45 minutes, Jesse Owens set or matched 6 world records.

SOURCE: DAVID WALLECHINSKY AND IRVING WALLACE. *THE PEOPLE'S ALMANAC #3*. BANTAM BOOKS, 1981.

First Successful Manned Space Flight

On April 12, 1961, Yuri Gagarin left the Soviet launching pad at Baykonur, Western Siberia, inside the 10,416-pound spaceship *Vostok 1*, on the world's first successful manned space flight. The spaceship completed a single orbit around the earth in 89.34 minutes and landed in a field near the village of Smelovka in the Saratov region of the USSR. SOURCE: IBID.

8 Stays of Execution

On May 2, 1960, Caryl Chessman entered the gas chamber at San Quentin prison after spending 11 years, 10 months, and 1 week on death row. He died after 8 minutes and 15 seconds. He holds a record of 8 stays of execution. SOURCE: IBID.

Pole to Pole

In April 1982, two British explorers reached the North Pole and became the first to circle the earth from pole to pole. They had reached the South Pole 16 months earlier. The 52,000-mile trek took 3 years, involved 23 people, and cost an estimated $18 million. SOURCE: *THE WORLD ALMANAC AND BOOK OF FACTS*, 1991.

First Implantation of Human Artificial Heart

On April 21, 1966, Michael E. DeBakey performed the first artificial heart implant operation in Houston, Texas. The plastic device functioned and the patient survived.

SOURCE: JOSEPH NATHAN KING. *FAMOUS FIRST FACTS*. WORLD BOOK, 1989.

First Oil Well

Edwin L. Drake drilled the first commercially productive oil well in Titusville, Pennsylvania, in 1859, starting the large-scale commercial exploitation of petroleum.

SOURCE: *1991 INFORMATION PLEASE ALMANAC*. HOUGHTON MIFFLIN.

Invention of the Solar Battery

The solar battery was developed by Bell Telephone Laboratories in 1954, making it possible to convert sunlight directly to electric power. SOURCE: *THE WORLD ALMANAC BOOK OF INVENTIONS, 1985*.

First Sewing Machine

In 1846, Elias Howe invented the lock switch sewing machine; and in 1851, Isaac M. Singer invented the first practical domestic sewing machine. SOURCE: IBID.

First Shaving Appliances

King C. Gillette invented the safety razor with throwaway blades in 1895. J. Schick invented the electric razor in 1928, and stainless steel throwaway blades were invented in Sweden in 1962. SOURCE: IAN GRAHAM. *INVENTIONS*. BOOKWRIGHT PRESS, 1987.

Ball-Point Pens Last

In 1938, Ladislao H. and George Biro patented the ball-point pen. SOURCE: IBID.

Stay Cool

In 1865, mechanical refrigeration was developed for the preservation of food.

SOURCE: *1991 INFORMATION PLEASE ALMANAC*. HOUGHTON MIFFLIN.

Where's Poppa?

In 1940, artificial insemination was developed to improve livestock breeding. SOURCE: IBID.

First Railroads in the United States

In 1829, the first railroads were opened up in the United States and France, both employing British-built locomotives. The first steam locomotive was built in 1830 by Peter Cooper.

SOURCE: DONALD CLARK. *THE ENCYCLOPEDIA OF INVENTIONS.* GALAHAD BOOKS, 1977.

First Calls

In 1876, Alexander Graham Bell patented the telephone. The first telephone exchange was installed in New Haven in 1877.

SOURCE: *1991 INFORMATION PLEASE ALMANAC.* HOUGHTON MIFFLIN.

First Cars

In 1885, Karl Benz produced the prototype of the automobile using an internal combustion motor operation on the Otto four-stroke cycle principle. That same year Gottlieb Daimler also patented his gasoline engine. The first automobile patent in the United States was taken out by George B. Seldon in 1879, but the Duryea in 1895 was the first automobile made for sale in the United States.

Henry Ford produced his first car in 1896 and founded the Ford Motor Company in 1903.

The first automatic transmission was perfected in 1939 by Earl A. Thompson. SOURCE: IBID.

First Motion Pictures

The first motion picture publicly shown was in Paris in 1895. It was not until 1926 that the first motion picture with sound was publicly shown, and in 1927 the first talking movie was shown.

SOURCE: MARC FERRO. *CINEMA AND HISTORY*. WAYNE STATE UNIVERSITY PRESS, 1988.

Instant Pictures

In 1947, Edwin H. Land invented the Polaroid Land camera, which developed the film inside the camera within 1 minute; in 1962 he developed color film for his camera.

SOURCE: RALPH STEIN. *THE GREAT INVENTIONS*. PLAYBOY PRESS, 1976.

For the Blind

Braille was invented in France in 1829 by Louis Braille.

SOURCE: DONALD CLARK. *THE ENCYCLOPEDIA OF INVENTIONS*. GALAHAD BOOKS, 1977.

Equivalence of Mass and Energy

Albert Einstein created his theory of relativity formula, $E = mc^2$, in Switzerland in 1907.

SOURCE: IBID.

First Parachute

Louis S. Lenormand invented the parachute in France in 1783.

SOURCE: IBID.

First Tractor

Benjamin Holt, an American, invented the first tractor in 1900.

SOURCE: *THE WOLRD ALMANAC BOOK OF INVENTIONS*, 1985.

First Commercial

On July 1, 1941, the world's first television commercial was broadcast by WNBT in New York City. A Bulova watch was shown on the screen while an announcer presented its features. The 10-second advertisement cost $9.

SOURCE: DAVID WALLECHINSKY AND IRVING WALLACE. *THE PEOPLE'S ALMANAC #3*. BANTAM BOOKS, 1981.

First American Accident Insurance Policy

In 1864, the Travelers Insurance Company sold the nation's first accident insurance policy to James Bolter. The $1,000 policy covered only the time Bolter spent walking from the post office to his home. The premium was 2 cents. SOURCE: IBID.

First Public School

Boston Latin School, which was founded in 1635, was the first public school in America. SOURCE: *WORLD BOOK ENCYCLOPEDIA*, 1989.

First Savings Bank

The Provident Institute for Savings in Boston, established in 1816, was the first U.S. savings bank.

SOURCE: JOSEPH NATHAN KANE. *FAMOUS FIRST FACTS*. WORLD BOOK, 1989.

First Skyscraper

Home Insurance Company, built in Chicago in 1885, was the first skyscraper in America with 10 floors. SOURCE: IBID.

First Slaves to America

A Dutch ship brought the first slaves to Jamestown, Virginia, in 1619. SOURCE: *1991 INFORMATION PLEASE ALMANAC*. HOUGHTON MIFFLIN.

First Subway

The first subway in America began operating in Boston in 1897. SOURCE: BENSON BOBRICK. *LABYRINTHS OF IRON, A HISTORY OF THE WORLD'S SUBWAYS*. NEWSWEEK BOOKS, 1981.

American Women in Space

The first female astronaut to be launched in space was Dr. Sally K. Ride in 1983. The first woman to walk in space was Dr. Kathryn D. Sullivan in 1984.

SOURCE: JANE HORWITZ. *SALLY RIDE, SHOOTING FOR THE STARS*. FAWCETT, 1989.

Women in Government

The first American women to hold government positions:
Governor: Nellie Tayloe/Ross of Wyoming in 1925.
Member of House of Representatives: Jeannette Rankin in 1916.
Member of U.S. Senate: Rebecca Latimer Felton of Georgia, appointed in 1922.
U.S. Supreme Court Member: Sandra Day O'Connor, appointed in 1981.

SOURCE: *1991 INFORMATION PLEASE ALAMANAC*. HOUGHTON MIFFLIN.

First Color Cartoon

"The Yellow Kid" by Richard Outcault was the first color cartoon in America. It appeared in the *New York World* in 1895.

SOURCE: JOSEPH NATHAN KANE. *FAMOUS FIRST FACTS*. WORLD BOOK, 1989.

First College in America

Harvard, founded in 1636, is the oldest university in America. SOURCE: IBID.

First Coed College

Oberlin College in Ohio, in 1833, became the first American coeducational college. SOURCE: IBID.

First Zap

The first criminal to be electrocuted was William Kemmler in Auburn Prison, Auburn, New York, on August 6, 1890.

SOURCE: IBID.

First Fraternity/Sorority

Phi Beta Kappa, founded on December 5, 1776, at the College of William and Mary, was the first fraternity. The first sorority was Kappa Alpha Theta at DePauw University in 1870.

SOURCE: IBID.

First Published Daily Newspaper

The first published daily newspaper was the *Pennsylvania Packet and General Advertiser* in Philadelphia, September 1784.

SOURCE: IBID.

First Issued Postage Stamps

Postage stamps were first issued in 1847.

SOURCE: IBID.

First American Colony

In 1607, the first American colony on the American mainland was permanently established in Jamestown, Virginia.

SOURCE: *1991 INFORMATION PLEASE ALMANAC*. HOUGHTON MIFFLIN.

First Birth in America to English Parents

Virginia Dare was the first person born in America to English parents. She was born on Roanoke Island, North Carolina, in 1587.

SOURCE: JOSEPH NATHAN KANE. *FAMOUS FIRST FACTS*. WORLD BOOK, 1989.

Patent of the Telegraph

In 1844, Samuel F. B. Morse received a patent for his invention of the telegraph.

SOURCE: DAVID C. COOKE. *INVENTIONS THAT MADE HISTORY*. PUTNAM, 1968.

Discovery of X Rays

In 1895, Wilhelm Roentgen, a German physicist, discovered X rays. SOURCE: RALPH STEIN. *THE GREAT INVENTIONS*. PLAYBOY PRESS, 1976.

First American to Orbit Earth

Lt. Col. John H. Glenn, Jr., on February 20, 1962, became the first American to orbit the earth. He orbited the earth 3 times in 4 hours and 55 minutes.

SOURCE: JOSEPH NATHAN KANE. *FAMOUS FIRST FACTS*. WORLD BOOK, 1989.

First Walk on the Moon

On July 20, 1969, *Apollo 11* astronauts Neil A. Armstrong and Edwin E. Aldrin, Jr. took man's first walk on the moon.

SOURCE: EDMOND L. LEIPOLD. *HEROES OF TODAY—THE ASTRONAUTS*. T. S. DENISON, 1973.

First Crossword Puzzle

On December 21, 1913, the first newspaper crossword puzzle in the United States was prepared by Arthur Wynne, and appeared in the *New York World*.

SOURCE: DAVID WALLECHINSKY AND IRVING WALLACE. *THE PEOPLE'S ALMANAC #2*. BANTAM BOOKS, 1978.

First Miss America

On September 7, 1921, the first beauty contest for the Miss America title, was held in Atlantic City, New Jersey. The first

Miss America was 15-year-old Margaret Gorman, a native of Washington, D.C. The petite 5 foot 1 inch blue-eyed blonde filled out her swimsuit at 30–25–32.

SOURCE: JOSEPH NATHAN KANE. *FAMOUS FIRST FACTS*. WORLD BOOK, 1989.

Don't Pass Go

In 1935, Parker Brothers of Salem, Massachusetts, marketed a new board game invented by Charles Darrow, an unemployed engineer. They named it *Monopoly*.

SOURCE: ELLEN WOJAHN. *PLAYING BY DIFFERENT RULES*. AMACOM, 1988.

First Canned Beer

On January 24, 1935, the American Can Company and the Gottfried Krueger Company of New Jersey manufactured the world's first canned beer, Krueger Cream Ale.

SOURCE: JOSEPH NATHAN KANE. *FAMOUS FIRST FACTS*. WORLD BOOK, 1989.

First-Time Home Buyers

The average first-time home buyer shops for an average of 5 months and looks at an average of 13 houses before he or she buys. The average cost of a first-time home was $133,700 in 1989. The new homeowner saves for an average of 3 years and pays an average of $969 a month on a 28-year mortgage. The average first-time buyer is 30 years old and has a pretax income of $50,700.

SOURCE: "WHO'S BUYING HOUSES IN AMERICA?"
CHICAGO TITLE AND TRUST COMPANY, 1990.

First Minimum Wage

The first minimum wage was established in 1939; it was 25 cents per hour.

SOURCE: BARBARA BERLINER, MELINDA COREY, AND GEORGE OCHOA.
THE BOOK OF ANSWERS. PRENTICE HALL PRESS, 1990.

First Heartbeats

A human embryo has its first heartbeat at the age of 3 weeks.

SOURCE: IBID.

First Leap Year

The first leap year was in 46 B.C. It was then that the Julian calendar of 365.25 days was adopted. The calendar required that an extra day be added every fourth year.

SOURCE: IBID.

First Strike in the United States

The first strike in the United States occurred in 1776, when members of the Journeymen Printers Union struck against their local shops in New York.

SOURCE: IBID.

The First American Express Travelers Cheque

In 1891, Marcellus F. Berry, an employee of American Express, was assigned to devise something that would be as safe as the letter of credit to be used by travelers. The result was the American Express Travelers Cheque, with its elegantly simple identification system of signature and countersignature. Almost $10,000 worth of Travelers Cheques were sold that year. By 1990, sales were in excess of $25 billion.

SOURCE: AMERICAN EXPRESS COMPANY.

The First Diners Card

In 1956, the first Diners Card was issued.

SOURCE: *PROMISES TO PAY*. AMERICAN EXPRESS COMPANY, 1977.

The First American Express Card

In 1958, the first American Express Card was issued. By the end of 1959, there were 600,000 cards in force. By 1962, there were 900,000 card members. In 1991, more than 37 million people around the world didn't leave home without it.

SOURCE: IBID.

Ye Ole Chop House

The Ye Ole Chop House was the first establishment to honor the American Express Card. This New York restaurant still accepts the card.

SOURCE: IBID.

Invention of Bifocals

In 1785, Benjamin Franklin invented bifocals because he hated carrying two pairs of glasses.

SOURCE: FRANK FOSTER AND ROBERT L. SHOOK. *PATENTS, COPYRIGHTS & TRADEMARKS*. WILEY, 1989.

First Woman to Get a Patent

On May 5, 1809, Mary Kies of Killingly, Connecticut, became the first American woman to receive a patent. Her invention was a device that wove straw with silk or thread.

SOURCE: IBID

Around the World Nonstop

The first nonstop round the world flight was made by Captain James Gallagher of Carswell AFB; the trip took 94 hours, 1 minute. The flight was completed on March 2, 1949, by the USAF's Boeing B-50 Superfortress *Lucky Lady II*; the aircraft refueled 4 times on its 23,452-mile voyage.

SOURCE: *GUINNESS BOOK OF WORLD RECORDS*, 1990.

Earliest Flights

Orville Wright made the first controlled and power-driven flight at 10:35 A.M. on December 17, 1903, on the 12-hp chain-driven *Flyer I* for a distance of 120 feet at an airspeed of 30 mph. His ground speed was 6.8 mph, and the aircraft reached an altitude of 8 to 12 feet, which it maintained for approximately 12 seconds.

The first international flight was across the English Channel on Sunday, July 25, 1909, when Louis Blériot of France flew his Blériot XI monoplane, powered by a 23-hp Anzani engine, 26 miles from Les Baraques, France, to Northfall Meadow near Dover Castle, England. The trip took 36½ minutes.

SOURCE: IBID.

American Inventions on the Rebound

In 1989, Americans received a larger share of the U.S.-issued patents than they had in 26 previous years. Inventors based in the United States obtained 54,762 patents.

SOURCE: THE PATENT AND TRADEMARK OFFICE.

Beneath the Arctic Ice

On August 3, 1958, the *Nautilus*, an atomic-powered submarine, under Commander William R. Anderson, became the first ship to cross the North Pole beneath the Arctic ice.

SOURCE: *THE WORLD ALMANAC AND BOOK OF FACTS*, 1991.

Breakthrough on the Top of the World

On August 16, 1977, the Soviet nuclear icebreaker *Arktika* reached the North Pole, becoming the first surface ship to break through the Arctic ice pack to the top of the world.

SOURCE: IBID.

First Bicycles

In 1867, Ernest Michaux invented the velocipede, the first bicycle with cranks placed directly on the front wheel; the "safety" bicycle with the geared chain-drive to the rear wheel was introduced in 1885.

SOURCE: *1991 INFORMATION PLEASE ALMANAC*. HOUGHTON MIFFLIN.

First U.S. Cenus

The Census Bureau took its first census in 1790 and counted 3.9 million people in the United States. Since then a census has been taken every 10 years for the past 200 years.

SOURCE: U.S. CENSUS BUREAU.

Origin of Paper

Paper gets its name from papyrus, an ancient writing material developed by the Egyptians about 4,000 years ago. It was not until about 2,000 years later that paper was invented by the Chinese.

SOURCE: *THE CAMBRIDGE ENCYCLOPEDIA.*

Invention of the Typewriter

The typewriter was invented in Italy in 1808 by Pellegrine Turri.

SOURCE: IBID.

First Human Gene Therapy

On September 14, 1990, a four-year-old girl became the first person to receive human gene therapy. During a 30-minute procedure, the patient was infused with about 1 billion white blood cells that had been outfitted through recombinant DNA technology with copies of the gene she lacked.

SOURCE: *THE WORLD ALMANAC AND BOOK OF FACTS*, 1991.

First Flight Across the Atlantic

On May 21, 1927, Charles Lindbergh landed at Le Bourget Airfield in Paris, becoming the first person to make a solo flight across the Atlantic Ocean. The 3,610-mile flight took 33 hours and 29½ minutes.

SOURCE: DAVID WALLECHINSKY AND IRVING WALLACE. *THE PEOPLE'S ALMANAC #3*. BANTAM BOOKS, 1981.

The First Time

The average American has intercourse for the first time between the ages of 16 and 17.

SOURCE: JUNE M. REINISCH. *THE KINSEY INSTITUTE NEW REPORT ON SEX.* ST. MARTIN'S PRESS, 1990.

First Cash Register

James Jake Ritty invented the cash register in 1879.

SOURCE: JOSEPH NATHAN KANE. *FAMOUS FIRST FACTS.* WORLD BOOK, 1989.

The First Commercial Computer

The first commercial computer was the Univac I, manufactured by the Remington Rand Corporation in Philadelphia, Pennsylvania, on June 14, 1951. It could retain 1,000 different numbers.

SOURCE: IBID.

Niagara Falls in a Barrel

Anna Edson Taylor was the first person to survive going over Niagara Falls in a barrel. She did it on October 24, 1901, in a 4½-foot high, 3-foot-in-diameter barrel. SOURCE: IBID.

Faster Than the Speed of Sound

The first supersonic flight was made on October 14, 1947, by Captain Charles Elwood Yeager, over Edwards Air Force Base, Muroc, California, in a U.S. Bell XS-1 rocket plane, with Mach 1.015 (670 mph) at an altitude of 42,000 feet.

SOURCE: *GUINNESS BOOK OF WORLD RECORDS*, 1990.

First Ice-Cream Cone

The first ice-cream cone was produced in 1896 by Italo Marchiony. He was granted a patent on December 1903.

SOURCE: INTERNATIONAL ICE CREAM ASSOCIATION.

First Neon Sign

The first neon sign blinked on at the Paris Motor Show on December 3, 1910. It was designed by physicist Georges Claude.

SOURCE: DAVID WALLECHINSKY AND IRVING WALLACE. *THE PEOPLE'S ALMANAC #2.* BANTAM BOOKS, 1978.

First Income Tax

Federal income tax was levied in the United States in 1913. It called for 1 percent of income above $3,000 for singles; and above $4,000 for married couples. A 1 percent surtax on incomes above $20,000 graduated to 6 percent for those individuals with earnings above $500,000. SOURCE: IBID

First Ford Sale

On July 15, 1903, the first Ford Motor Company production car, a two-cylinder Model A, was sold to Ernst Pfenning, a Chicago dentist. The price was $850.

SOURCE: ROBERT L. SHOOK. *TURNAROUND: THE NEW FORD MOTOR COMPANY.* PRENTICE HALL PRESS, 1990.

First Assembly Line

Henry Ford, the father of mass production in America, produced the first Model T in 1911 in 12.5 hours. His ambition was to build 1 car every minute. By 1913, the production time per car was reduced to 1 hour and 33 minutes. By 1920, he surpassed his goal of producing cars at the rate of 1 per minute. By 1925, his company was producing cars at the rate of 1 every 10 seconds. SOURCE: IBID.

America's First Billionaire

Henry Ford, the founder of Ford Motor Company, was the nation's first billionaire. He achieved this status in 1915, when a billion dollars was really an enormous sum! SOURCE: IBID.

Henry Ford and Henry Ford II

Henry Ford, the founder of Ford Motor Company, and his grandson, Henry Ford II, were CEOs of the company for 75 consecutive years (1903–1978), the longest family reign of a major U.S. corporation. SOURCE: IBID.

The First Patents

One of the earliest references to patents is a message by the third-century Greek historian Phylarchus in the *Banquet of the Learned*. Phylarchus writes about Sybaris, a Greek colony that was famous in 500 B.C. for luxurious living and self-indulgence. The historian states that if a confectioner or cook invented an unusual or outstanding dish, no other artist was allowed to prepare it for a period of 1 year. The granting of a monopoly thereby served as an inducement to others "to labour at excelling in such pursuits." SOURCE: FRANK FOSTER AND ROBERT L. SHOOK. *PATENTS, COPYRIGHTS & TRADEMARKS*. WILEY, 1989.

The First Patent in the Western Hemisphere

In 1641, the colony of Massachusetts granted the first patent in the western hemisphere to Samuel Winslow for his invention of a process for manufacturing salt. The first American patent for machinery was issued by the Massachusetts Colony in 1646 to Joseph Jenkes for his invention of "engines of mills to go by water." SOURCE: IBID.

The First U.S. Patent

On April 10, 1790, a patent bill was passed by both houses of Congress. President Washington signed the first patent act. A separate copyright act was enacted on May 31, 1790. When the first U.S. patent was issued that year, George Washington and Thomas Jefferson actually signed it. SOURCE: IBID.

History of Number of Patents Issued in the United States

In 1790, the U.S. Patent Office issued 3. In 1791, 33 were issued, and then only 11 in 1792, and the number slipped back to 10 in 1793. The number of patents issued in the United States has increased dramatically in the twentieth century. In 1935, patent number 2 million was issued, and in 1961, patent number 3 million was issued. As of 1989, more than 4.7 million have been issued.

SOURCE: IBID.

First Copyright

The need for copyright protection originated in England and did not become widespread until 1476. This was the year when William Caxton became England's first printer and opened his shop in Westminster. The Crown became concerned that the new and growing trade of printing and book selling would wrongly influence the public with dangerous political and religious ideas. With this thought in mind, the government recognized the need to regulate the printing industry in order to maintain a strong grip (censorship) on what was written.

SOURCE: IBID.

U.S. Trademarks

In 1870, the first federal trademark act was enacted and 121 trademarks were registered. By 1970, a century later, 23,447 federal registrations were granted and 33,326 applications filed. By 1989, more than 1,560,000 federal registrations had been issued, although many are now abandoned or canceled. The widespread use of trademarks has become an essential part of modern business.

SOURCE: IBID.

The First McDonald's

Dick and Mac McDonald opened the first McDonald's drive-in restaurant in December 1948 in San Bernardino, California.

The first franchise was opened by Ray Kroc on April 15, 1955, in Des Plaines, Illinois. Opening-day sales totaled $366.12.

SOURCE: MCDONALD'S CORPORATION.

Ferris Wheel

The Ferris wheel was first used at the 1893 World's Columbian Exposition in Chicago. It was invented by George W. G. Ferris, an American railroad and bridge engineer.

SOURCE: *COUNRY LIVING*, MAY 1990.

First Supermarket in United States

In 1916, Clarence Saunders started up his Piggley Wiggley self-service food mart in Memphis, Tennessee, the nation's first supermarket. SOURCE: *PROGRESSIVE GROCER*.

The First Old Farmer's Almanac

The Old Farmer's Almanac was published for the first time in September 1771. It has not changed its cover since 1851.

SOURCE: *THE OLD FARMER'S ALMANAC*.

First-Time Smokers

Every day, 3,000 teenagers light up a cigarette for the first time. SOURCE: AMERICAN CANCER SOCIETY.

3. *How Much Time Does It Take?*

4-Year Universities?

Only 1 student in 6 finishes college in 4 years. After 6 years about 40 percent have a degree and about 15 percent are still in school pursuing one.

SOURCE: NATIONAL INSTITUTE OF INDEPENDENT COLLEGES AND UNIVERSITIES.

Arriving on Schedule

79.6 percent of flights by the largest U.S. carriers arrived on time during the month of September 1989; that is, within 15 minutes of schedule. SOURCE: DEPARTMENT OF TRANSPORTATION.

Job Hunting

Percentage of executives in different salary ranges whose job searches took:

	UP TO 6 MONTHS	6 TO 12 MONTHS	OVER 1 YEAR
Up to $50,000	89%	11%	—
$50,000–$100,000	53%	39%	8%
$100,000–$150,000	36%	46%	18%
$150,000–$200,000	38%	50%	12%
Over $200,000	33%	33%	33%

SOURCE: POLSON & COMPANY.

In 30 Minutes or Less . . .

The odds are 9 to 1 that your pizza will be delivered by Domino's in less than 30 minutes. SOURCE: DOMINO'S PIZZA.

Postgraduation Gap

The time between graduation from college and the awarding of a Ph.D. has lengthened by 30 percent during the past 20 years, with the average gap now ranging from about 7.4 years in the physical sciences to 16.2 years in education.

SOURCE: NATIONAL RESEARCH COUNCIL.

U.S. Population Growth Patterns

With about 250 million people, the United States ranks fourth among all nations, which is 10.4 percent higher than the 1980 census of 226,545,805.

The first census in 1790 counted fewer than 4 million Americans. The population in 1880 was 50 million, 100 million in 1915, 150 million in 1949, and 200 million in 1967.

Projections show the U.S. population could reach 300 million by about 2020. Every day the population increases by about 6,300, with a 4,400 surplus of births over deaths. The rest comes from immigration. The net gain of 1 person every 14 seconds is based on 1 birth every 8 seconds, 1 death every 14 seconds,

1 immigrant every 35 seconds, and 1 person leaving the country every 3 minutes.

SOURCE: U.S. CENSUS BUREAU AND AUTHORS' CALCULATIONS.

Rolls-Royces Take a Long Time to Build

It takes about 6 months to build a Rolls-Royce.

SOURCE: ROLLS-ROYCE MOTOR CARS INC.

Design to Showroom

Toyota takes a new car design from concept to showroom in less than 4 years. Mercedes-Benz takes about 7 years to complete a new design.

SOURCE: "TOYOTA VS. THE COMPETITION," *FORTUNE*, NOVEMBER 19, 1990, P. 72.

Close to Work

18 percent of American workers live within 10 minutes of work. 52 percent live within 20 minutes of work.

SOURCE: 1980 CENSUS OF POPULATION: GENERAL SOCIAL AND ECONOMIC CHARACTERISTICS, UNITED STATES SUMMARY. BUREAU OF THE CENSUS. U.S. DEPARTMENT OF COMMERCE.

Getting a Patent

The average patent pendency time in 1988 was 19.9 months. Of the 148,183 patent applications that year, 83,594 were issued. About 45 percent of the applications were from foreign residents and about 47 percent of them were issued.

SOURCE: U.S. DEPARTMENT OF COMMERCE, PATENT AND TRADEMARK OFFICE.

Getting a Trademark

In 1988, 76,813 applications were submitted for trademarks and 52,461 were registered in an average time of about 13 months.

SOURCE: IBID.

Average Patent Search

The average patent search takes about 15 hours.

SOURCE: FRANK FOSTER AND ROBERT L. SHOOK. *PATENTS, COPYRIGHTS & TRADEMARKS*. WILEY, 1989.

Legally Drunk

A person who weighs 150 pounds and has had little or no food intake needs to consume about 5 ounces of 80-proof liquor in 1 hour to reach a blood-alcohol level of .10. 5 ounces of alcohol is the equivalent of 4 12-ounce cans of beer or 4 4-ounce glasses of wine.

SOURCE: U.S. DEPARTMENT OF HEALTH AND HUMAN SERVICES.

What's in a Puff?

When the average American woman puffs a cigarette, each drag lasts 1.49 seconds. She puffs every 25 seconds, and gets 11½ puffs per cigarette. Altogether, her cigarette lasts 4 minutes, 29 seconds.

The average American male's puff lasts a little longer—1.7 seconds, and he waits 26 seconds between puffs. He gets only 10.9 drags from a cigarette, but it lasts him 4 minutes, 34 seconds. In an average year, a pack-a-day cigarette smoker takes 50,000 to 70,000 puffs.

SOURCE: MIKE FEINSILBER AND WILLIAM B. MEAD. *AMERICAN AVERAGES*. DOUBLEDAY, 1980.

Growing Hair

Hair grows an average of about 1 inch every 8 weeks.

SOURCE: KENNETH ROSE. *THE BODY IN TIME*. WILEY, 1989.

Growing Nails

It takes about a year for fingernails to grow an inch and about 4 years for toenails to grow an inch.

SOURCE: IBID.

A Journey Around the Sun

The Earth: The earth makes 1 absolute revolution around the sun in 365 days, 6 hours, 9 minutes, and 9.5 seconds.

Jupiter: Jupiter is almost 480 million miles from the sun and takes about 12 years to complete 1 circuit of the sun.

Mars: Mars takes about 687 days to make 1 circuit of the sun, traveling at about 15 miles a second.

Mercury: Mercury makes a full circuit around the sun in 88 days, traveling at about 30 miles a second.

Neptune: Neptune orbits the sun in 164 years in nearly a circular orbit.

Pluto: Pluto takes 247.7 years to circle the sun.

Uranus: Uranus lies a distance of 1.8 billion miles from the sun, taking 84 years to circle around it.

Venus: Venus moves about the sun at a mean distance of 67 million miles in 225 of our days.

SOURCE: *THE WORLD ALMANAC AND BOOK OF FACTS*, 1991.

Extreme Seasons

Uranus has very extreme seasons. When the sun rises at the north pole of this planet, it stays up for 42 years; then it sets and the north pole remains in darkness (and winter) for 42 years.

SOURCE: IBID.

Around the Earth in Less Than a Month

The moon completes a circuit around the earth in a period whose mean or average duration is 27 days, 7 hours, and 43.2 minutes.

SOURCE: IBID.

The Lunar Month

The lunar month is the duration of time between one new moon to the next new moon, which is 29 days, 12 hours, and 44.05 minutes. This is the moon's synodical period.

SOURCE: IBID.

The Cosmic Year

The cosmic year is the time it takes the sun to complete one revolution around the center of the Milky Way, which is about 225 million earth years. The sun is between 20 to 21 cosmic years old.

SOURCE: BARBARA BERLINER, MELINDA COREY, AND GEORGE OCHOA. *THE BOOK OF ANSWERS*. PRENTICE HALL PRESS, 1990.

Continental Drift

Europe and North America are drifting apart from each other at a rate of about 2 centimeters per year. The plates that are mostly under oceans move faster, at an average speed of 10 centimeters per year. It has been 200 million years since the original supercontinent, Pangaea, broke up into the continents we know today.

SOURCE: IBID.

Movie Sequels

Movies with the longest stretch between the first release and the sequel:

International Velvet, the sequel to *National Velvet*, opened 34 years after the original.

The Hustler opened in 1961, its sequel, *The Color of Money*, 25 years later in 1986.

Psycho opened in 1960 and its sequel, *Psycho II*, opened in 1983, 23 years later.

Texasville, the sequel to *The Last Picture Show*, opened 19 years after the original.

SOURCE: *GUINNESS FILM FACTS & FEATS* AND *USA TODAY* RESEARCH.

The Erie Canal

The Erie Canal was begun in 1817 and completed in 1825. It was the first major American civil engineering feat.

SOURCE: *1991 INFORMATION PLEASE ALMANAC*. HOUGHTON MIFFLIN.

St. Peter's Church

The construction of St. Peter's Church in Rome began in 1506. It was designed and decorated by such artists and architects as Bramante, Michelangelo, da Vinci, Raphael, and Bernini before its completion in 1626. SOURCE: IBID.

The Bubonic Plague

From 1347 to 1351 at least 25 million people died from Europe's "Black Death." SOURCE: IBID.

Transformation of Latin Bible to English

It took about 6 years, from 1376 to 1382, for John Wycliffe, a pre-Reformation religious reformer and his followers to translate the Latin Bible into English. SOURCE: IBID.

Statue of Liberty

The exterior copper shell of the classical female figure, carrying a torch aloft, was designed in 1870 to 1875 by the French sculptor Frédéric-Auguste Bartholdi.

SOURCE: *ACADEMIC AMERICAN ENCYCLOPEDIA*, 1985.

Eiffel Tower

The Eiffel Tower, completed in 1889, took 26½ months to complete; the elevators were installed later.

SOURCE: *ENCYCLOPEDIA AMERICANA INTERNATIONAL EDITION*, 1989.

Brooklyn Bridge

The construction of the Brooklyn Bridge began in 1869, but the bridge was not opened until May 1883. SOURCE; IBID.

Crystal Palace

Joseph Paxton built the Crystal Palace for the first World's Fair, the Great Exhibition of 1851. It was the largest building at that time and was completed in only 6 months. This enormous transparent box of 117,000 square yards burned down in 1936.

SOURCE: J. J. NORWICH. *THE ATLAS OF ARCHITECTURE*. PORLAND HOUSE, 1988.

Wells Cathedral

Wells Cathedral construction began between 1183 and 1192 and was not finished until 1260. SOURCE: IBID.

Constantinople

A new wall to protect Constantinople was constructed between 413 and 440, and was begun by Theodosius II.

SOURCE: IBID.

The British Museum, London

The British Museum was built between 1823 and 1847 by the architect Robert Smirke. SOURCE: IBID.

World Trade Center

The World Trade Center was built by Minoru Yamasaki from 1969 to 1974. It is 1,378 feet high with 104 stories.

SOURCE: IBID.

Biggest Tomb Ever Built

Shah Jahan built the Taj Mahal to house the remains of his favorite queen, Mumtaz Mahal. This building at Agra, India, was built between 1632 and 1647. SOURCE: IBID.

Empire State Building

The Empire State Building was built between 1930 and 1932 by Shreve, Lamb & Harmon. At the time it was the tallest building in the world.

SOURCE: RICHARD REID. *THE BOOK OF BUILDINGS*. RAND MCNALLY, 1980.

Sistine Chapel

The Sistine Chapel was built between 1473 and 1481 by Giovanni De Dorci; Michelangelo Buonarroti painted the barrel-vaulted ceiling between 1508 and 1512 and the altar wall from 1534 to 1541.

SOURCE: IBID.

Tribune Tower

The Tribune Tower in Chicago was built between 1922 and 1925.

SOURCE: IBID.

Water Tower

The Water Tower on Michigan Avenue, Chicago, was built between 1867 and 1869.

SOURCE: IBID.

Great Chicago Fire

The great Chicago fire on October 8, 1871, lasted 27 hours, killed 250 people, and destroyed 17,450 buildings!

SOURCE: BARBARA BERLINER, MELINDA COREY, AND GEORGE OCHOA. *THE BOOK OF ANSWERS*. PRENTICE HALL PRESS, 1990.

Dispose of Magazines

The average magazine is read by 4 people for a total of 6 hours, 3 minutes, and it sits around the house for 29 weeks before someone throws it out.

SOURCE: MAGAZINE PUBLISHERS ASSOCIATION.

School Days

The average number of days in the U.S. school year is 180. This compares with 180 in Sweden and Mexico. Belgium has 160; Scotland has 200; Israel 215; South Korea 220; and Japan has 243.

SOURCE: NATIONAL ASSOCIATION OF ELEMENTARY SCHOOL PRINCIPALS.

Man-Hours to Assemble Automobile

It takes Toyota only 13 man-hours to assemble a car in its best plant. Honda and Nissan cars require 19 to 22 hours.

SOURCE: "TOYOTA VS. THE COMPETITION," *FORTUNE*, NOVEMBER 19, 1990. P. 72.

Calling AAA

The average time lapse between a reported call and the arrival of an AAA service person is 25 minutes.

SOURCE: AMERICAN AUTOMOBILE ASSOCIATION.

Time to Change Clocks

It takes the average person about 7 minutes to change his or her average of 6 clocks. It takes Main Street USA at Disney World's Magic Kingdom about 2 hours to change its 6 clocks. And it takes about 2 hours to change the 1 clock at Independence Hall in Philadelphia. SOURCE: *USA TODAY* RESEARCH.

Santa Speeds . . .

Based on the estimated population of North America and Europe on December 24, 1991, there are 42,466,666 homes that Santa Claus must visit within a 12-hour period to deliver toys to the children whose families celebrate Christmas. If every boy and girl is to receive a gift, Santa must stop at 983 homes per second. Well, Virginia, what do you think now?

SOURCE: CALCULATED BY STEPHEN SAUPE, COLLEGE OF ST. BENEDICT, ST. JOSEPH, MINNESOTA.

The Mayflower Voyage

Early in September 1620, the *Mayflower* sailed from Plymouth, England, arriving after 65 treacherous days at sea at the tip of Cape Cod where Provincetown, Massachusetts, now stands.

SOURCE: *BRITANNICA JUNIOR ENCYCLOPEDIA*, 1971.

How Long Will It Take to Decompose?

It takes 2 to 4 weeks for a traffic ticket to decompose.
A cotton rag takes 1 to 5 months.
A plastic 6-pack ring takes more than 450 years.
An aluminum can can take as much as 200 to 500 years.

SOURCE: WASHINGTON CITIZENS FOR RECYCLING.

Hitting the Accelerator

COMPACT SEDANS	
Toyota Corolla	0–60 mph in 11.3 seconds
Ford Escort	0–60 mph in 10.5 seconds
Honda Civic	0–60 mph in 9.6 seconds

SPORTY COUPES	
Toyota Celica	0–60 mph in 9.5 seconds
Ford Probe	0–60 mph in 7.2 seconds
Plymouth Laser	0–60 mph in 8.8 seconds

MIDSIZE SEDANS	
Toyota Camry	0–60 mph in 11.5 seconds
Honda Accord	0–60 mph in 10.0 seconds

TWO-SEATERS UNDER $20,000	
Toyota MR2	0–60 mph in 8.5 seconds
Mazda Miata	0–60 mph in 9.4 seconds
Mazda RX7	0–60 mph in 9.2 seconds

LUXURY SEDANS	
Lexus LS 400	0–60 mph in 8.1 seconds
Cadillac Deville	0–60 mph in 8.8 seconds
BMW 535i	0–60 mph in 8.9 seconds

SOURCE: *FORTUNE*, NOVEMBER 19, 1990, PP. 70–71.

4. People Patterns

Frequency of Sex

45 percent of married couples, 61 percent of cohabitating couples, 33 percent of lesbian duos, and 67 percent of gay men pairs who have been together up to 2 years have sex at least 3 times a week. 18 percent of married couples, 1 percent of lesbians, and 11 percent of gay men together for 10 years or more have sex at least 3 times a week. 15 percent of married couples, 47 percent of lesbians, and 33 percent of gay men together for 10 years or more have sex once a month or less.

SOURCE: PHILIP BLUMSTEIN AND PEPPER SCHWARTZ. *AMERICAN COUPLES*. POCKET BOOKS, 1985.

Sex Over 80

Among healthy, upper-middle-class whites ages 80 to 102, 30 percent of females and 63 percent of males have sexual intercourse and 20 percent of females and 72 percent of males masturbate. SOURCE: *ARCHIVES OF SEXUAL BEHAVIOR*, APRIL 1988.

Favorite Time to Have Sex

32 percent of men favor having sex in the morning compared with 21 percent of women. 10 percent of men favor having sex

in the afternoon compared with 16 percent of women. 52 percent of men favor having sex in the evening compared with 49 percent of females, and 6 percent of men favor having sex after midnight compared with 14 percent of women.

SOURCE: MEL PORETZ AND BARRY SINROD. *THE FIRST REALLY IMPORTANT SURVEY OF AMERICAN HABITS*. PRICE, STERN, SLOAN, 1989.

Sex in Their Twenties and Thirties

The average American couple in their twenties and thirties has sex two or three times a week. SOURCE: THE KINSEY INSTITUTE.

Planned First Intercourse

17 percent of females and 25 percent of males planned their first intercourse.[1] 40 percent of females and 60 percent of males tell somebody within a month about their first coital experiences, and 40 percent of females and 67 percent of males say their parents knew about their first coital experiences.[2]

SOURCE:[1] TOM AND NANCY BIRACREE. *ALMANAC OF THE AMERICAN PEOPLE*. FACTS ON FILE, 1988.
[2] KATHRYN KELLEY, ED. *FEMALES, MALES, AND SEXUALITY*. STATE UNIVERSITY OF NEW YORK PRESS. 1987.

Kissing Couples

95 percent of lesbians, 71 percent of gay men, and 80 percent of heterosexuals kiss every time they have sex.

SOURCE: PHILIP BLUMSTEIN AND PEPPER SCHWARTZ. *AMERICAN COUPLES*. POCKET BOOKS, 1985.

Average Age for First-Time Intercourse in the United States

The average age of first intercourse is 17.2 for females and 16.5 for males. By age 20, 3 out of 4 females and 5 out of 6 males will have had sexual intercourse at least once, as will 1 in 6 15-year-old males and 1 in 20 15-year-old females.

SOURCE: ANN LANDERS, UNIVERSAL PRESS SYNDICATE.

Sex After 60

More than 65 percent of couples over 60 years old and 75 percent of couples over 70 have infrequent or no sex.

SOURCE: ANN LANDERS, *COLUMBUS* (OHIO) *DISPATCH*, JUNE 25, 1990.

Reaching Menopause

The average woman reaches menopause anywhere from age 48 to 52.

SOURCE: *MASTERS AND JOHNSON ON SEX AND HUMAN LOVING*. LITTLE, BROWN, 1986.

Getting Around

The average adult has 1.16 sexual partners a year.

SOURCE: NATIONAL OPINION RESEARCH CENTER, UNIVERSITY OF CHICAGO.

Cohabitation Yields Higher Divorce Rates

10 years after marriage, 53 percent of those who had cohabitated before marriage had divorced. 28 percent of those who had never cohabitated had divorced.

SOURCE: *SOCIETY*, JULY/AUGUST 1988.

Widowed and Old Age

49 percent of females and 14 percent of males age 65 and over are widowed.[1] 67 percent of females and 24 percent of males age 75 and over are widowed, and 52 percent of females and 22 percent of males over the age of 75 live alone.[2]

SOURCES: [1] *STATISTICAL ABSTRACT OF THE UNITED STATES 1989*. BUREAU OF THE CENSUS.

[2] *POPULATION BULLETIN*, SEPTEMBER 1988.

Military Marry Early

The median age at first marriage for U.S. Army men is 20.7 years, versus 25.5 years for civilians. SOURCE: RAND CORPORATION.

Vows Taken

63 percent of Americans 18 years or older are married.

SOURCE: *STATISTICAL ABSTRACT OF THE UNITED STATES 1987*. BUREAU OF THE CENSUS. U.S. DEPARTMENT OF COMMERCE.

Single Adults

2 out of 25 Americans 18 years or older are divorced. The same figures apply to widowed persons. SOURCE: IBID.

Age of Marriage

	MEDIAN AGE AT MARRIAGE (YEARS)	
	BRIDE	GROOM
Both first marriage	21.8	23.9
Bride's first, groom's remarriage	25.4	31.9
Groom's first, bride's remarriage	28.6	27.1
Both remarried	35.6	39.1

SOURCE: NCHS DATA ON MARRIAGES IN 1986. COMPILED BY BENCHMARK DATA SERVICES, HAMILTON, MONTANA.

Fast-Food Consumption

$230 per capita was spent on fast food in the United States during 1988. SOURCE: *RESTAURANT BUSINESS*.

Billions of Coupons

Although Americans use 7 billion coupons a year—saving some $3 billion—about 97 percent of all coupons circulated go unused. SOURCE: *BUYER'S BULLETIN*, PUBLISHED BY BUYER'S MARKET, A SERVICE OF EQUIFAX CONSUMER DIRECT, WASHINGTON, D.C.

Lick It Down

The average Southerner eats 12 quarts of ice cream each year. The average New Englander eats about 23 quarts per year.

SOURCE: INTERNATIONAL ASSOCIATION OF ICE CREAM MANUFACTURERS, WASHINGTON, D.C.

Ice Cream Consumption

Nearly one-third of American households consume at least 1 gallon of ice cream and related products every 2 weeks. U.S. ice cream consumption is highest in June and July (National Ice Cream Month).

SOURCE: IBID.

How Much We Eat Each Year

The average American consumes 1,417 pounds of food each year.

SOURCE: U.S. DEPARTMENT OF AGRICULTURE.

Dining Out

35 out of 100 Americans go out for dinner at least once a week.

SOURCE: *AMERICA IN THE EIGHTIES.* R. H. BRUSKIN ASSOCIATES MARKET RESEARCH, 1985.

Home Delivery

2 out of 5 Americans had pizza delivered to them in the last 3 months.

SOURCE: LEWIS LAPHAM, MICHAEL POLLAN, ERIC WETHERIDGE. *THE HARPER'S INDEX.* HENRY HOLT, 1987.

Starting Off the Day

41 out of 100 Americans eat cereal for breakfast every day.

SOURCE: *STATISTICAL ABSTRACT OF THE UNITED STATES 1987.* BUREAU OF THE CENSUS. U.S. DEPARTMENT OF COMMERCE.

2 to 3 Meals a Day

34 percent of females and 40 percent of males eat 2 meals a day. 53 percent of females and 48 percent of males eat 3 meals a day. SOURCE: *SURVEY OF AMERICAN ADULTS*. KANE, PARSONS AND ASSOCIATES. *PARENTS MAGAZINE*, NOVEMBER 1987.

Quick Dining

One-fifth of us eat at a fast-food restaurant each day.
SOURCE: WENDY'S GALLUP SURVEY OF 1,029 FAST-FOOD CONSUMERS.

Big Mac Attack

1 out of 20 Americans eats at a McDonald's every day.
SOURCE; "FASCINATING MCFACTS," MCDONALD'S CORPORATION, 1984.

Total Alcohol Consumption

Total alcohol consumption was about 40.6 gallons per person in 1987. SOURCE: *STATISTICAL ABSTRACT OF THE UNITED STATES 1987.*

Wacky Tobacky

1 out of 3 Americans has tried marijuana at least once in his or her life. SOURCE: "NIDA CAPSULES," NATIONAL INSTITUTE ON DRUG ABUSE, NOVEMBER 1986.

A Pack Plus a Day

13 percent of female and 25 percent of male smokers smoke more than a pack a day.
SOURCE: GEORGE GALLUP, JR. *THE GALLUP POLL: PUBLIC OPINION 1988.*

Serious Drinking

20 percent of females and 30 percent of males occasionally consume 5 or more drinks at each sitting.

SOURCE: TOM AND NANCY BIRACREE. *ALMANAC OF THE AMERICAN PEOPLE*. FACTS ON FILE, 1988.

On the Wagon

2 percent of females and 3 percent of males gave up drinking in the past year.

SOURCE: *ROPER REPORTS*, FEBRUARY 1989.

Drinking Habits

32 percent of all Americans consume no more than 3 drinks per week. 22 percent of all Americans have no more than 2 drinks a day. 11 percent of all Americans have more than 2 drinks per day.

SOURCE: INSTITUTE OF MEDICINE, AN AGENCY OF THE NATIONAL ACADEMY OF SCIENCES.

Daily Reading

54 percent of females and 57 percent of males read a newspaper almost every day.

SOURCE: *AMERICA IN THE EIGHTIES*. R. H. BRUSKIN ASSOCIATES MARKET RESEARCH, 1985.

Combing Magazines

The average American reads 36 magazines per year.

SOURCE: 1990 CENSUS STATISTICS.

Readers of the Good Book

1 out of 10 Americans reads the Bible every day.

SOURCE: GEORGE GALLUP, JR. *THE GALLUP POLL: PUBLIC OPINION 1986*. SCHOLARLY RESOURCES, INC.

Pick Up a Book!

44 percent of American adults did not read a book in the course of a year. SOURCE: U.S. DEPARTMENT OF EDUCATION.

Buy a Book

Approximately 93 million people visit a bookstore at least once a month and about half purchase a book.

SOURCE: AMERICAN BOOKSELLERS ASSOCIATION.

Going to College

34 percent of females and 41 percent of males age 25 and over finished at least 1 year of college.

17 percent of females and 24 percent of males age 25 and over finished at least 4 years of college.

5 percent of females and 9 percent of males age 25 and over finished at least 5 years of college.

SOURCE: *EDUCATIONAL ATTAINMENT IN THE UNITED STATES: MARCH 1987 AND 1986*. CURRENT POPULATION REPORTS. POPULATION CHARACTERISTICS. BUREAU OF THE CENSUS.

Japanese College Students Have It Easy

Japanese college students attend classes and study far less than their American counterparts. About 53 percent of Japanese students say they study 2 hours or less each day and about 37 percent say they don't study at all. On the other hand, 30 percent of American students say they study in libraries and at home 7 hours a day or longer; 26 percent say they study 2 hours a day or less and only .5 percent said they don't study at all.

Japanese students also spend less time in class or at laboratories. 36 percent of U.S. students say they spend 7 hours each day at school, whereas only 9.8 percent of Japanese students say they spend that much time at class or lab. Only 8 percent of American students spend 2 hours or less in the classroom or lab a day; among Japanese students the figure was 15 percent.

SOURCE: GAKUSEI ENGO-KAI, PUBLISHER OF A JOB PLACEMENT MAGAZINE IN TOKYO.

Educational Levels in United States

In 1990, of all adults age 25 and older, 77.3 percent were high-school graduates, 18.6 percent were college graduates, and 20.3 percent completed 4 or more years of college.

SOURCE: *AMERICAN DEMOGRAPHICS'* ESTIMATES.

Flight Time

An estimated 75 percent of all Americans have flown at least once, and 30 percent of these travelers fly at least 3 times a year. SOURCE: PETER D. HART RESEARCH AND ASSOCIATES.

Busiest Airports

	TOTAL PASSENGERS IN 1989
1. Chicago (O'Hare), IL	25,664,266
2. Dallas/Ft. Worth (Regional), TX	22,623,065
3. Atlanta, GA	20,397,697
4. Los Angeles, CA	18,583,292
5. San Francisco, CA	13,326,085

SOURCE: AIRPORT ACTIVITY STATISTICS OF CERTIFICATED ROUTE AIR CARRIERS, FAA, 1989.

Going to Atlantic City

Although the odds of winning at the gaming tables in Atlantic City aren't in your favor, the odds of going there are. More people will visit this New Jersey gambling community than any other place in the United States. 33 million people visit Atlantic City each year, or 1 out of 7 Americans.

SOURCE: *TIME*, SEPTEMBER 25, 1989.

Cruisin'

An estimated 5 percent of all Americans go on a cruise each year. Of these tourists, 33 percent visit the Caribbean. Evidently Americans love cruises—9 out of 10 go cruisin' again.

SOURCE: CRUISELINER ASSOCIATION.

Experienced Riders

The average motorcycle owner has been riding for 8 years and has owned 3 cycles.

SOURCE: 1985 SURVEY OF MOTORCYCLE OWNERSHIP AND USAGE.

Who Comes to the United States?

(Top 10 visiting nationals to the United States in thousands)

COUNTRY OF ORIGIN	NUMBER OF VISITORS
Canada	12,418
Mexico	6,705
Japan	2,128
United Kingdom	1,362
West Germany	952
France	544
Italy	319
Australia	278
Switzerland	239
Brazil	239

SOURCE: U.S. TRAVEL AND TOURISM ADMINISTRATION, 1987.

Staying Put

In 1989, the average homeowner had remained in his or her home exactly 12 years. SOURCE: CHICAGO TITLE & TRUST CO.

Our Country Cousins

100 years ago, 66 percent of Americans lived in rural areas. By 1950, there were only 36 percent, and today, it's 27 percent. Just 2 percent of Americans live on farms today versus 15 percent in 1950 and nearly 40 percent in 1880.

SOURCE: *WALL STREET JOURNAL*, DECEMBER 30, 1990; COMPILED BY STAFF OF *AMERICAN DEMOGRAPHICS*.

Lives in the Big City(s)

Los Angeles, the nation's second largest metropolitan area, second to New York City, had a population increase of 26.4 percent between 1980 and 1990. Its 1980 population was 11,497,549 and increased by 3,033,980 in 10 years to 14,531,529. This means an increase of 831 people each day, or about 35 per hour! New York's population increased from 17,539,532 to 18,087,251 during the same 10-year period. The Big Apple's 3.1 percent jump represents 150 people a day, or roughly 6 people per hour. SOURCE: U.S. CENSUS BUREAU.

California, Here I Come

California, the most populous state in the union, keeps getting more and more people. During the 1980s, its population increased by 6.1 million (that's 13 times the population of Wyoming, the least populous state). This means that, on a daily basis, 1,671 people were born in or moved to California, or about 70 per hour. That's more than 1 per minute, around the clock, 24 hours a day, 365 days a year. SOURCE: U.S. CENSUS BUREAU.

Book Buyers in the United States

Only 2 of every 5 U.S. households bought a book in the year from April 1990 through March 1991. Two-thirds of all books bought were fiction, and sales in this category increased with the age of readers. People older than 65 were the largest group of book buyers, accounting for 16 percent of sales.

SOURCE: A SURVEY MADE BY THE AMERICAN BOOKSELLERS ASSOCIATION OF AMERICAN PUBLISHERS IN COLLABORATION WITH THE BOOK INDUSTRY STUDY GROUP.

The Big Move to Nevada

Nevada's population was the fastest growing between 1980 and 1989, increasing more than 39 percent. Biggest loser: West Virginia with a 5 percent drop. SOURCE: U.S. CENSUS BUREAU.

Sexy Leisure Time Activities

A 1991 study titled *At Our Leisure*, reveals that the sexiest leisure activities enjoyed by married couples are showering together (43 Americans bathe with their spouses); watching X-rated videos (24.5 million Americans do so); sneaking off to hotels together to be alone (38 million Americans do this); and making love outdoors (24 million Americans say they've done this at least once). SOURCE: RESEARCH ALERT.

Senior Management

Nearly a third of the executives surveyed in 1989 said they wish to retire before age 60. Age 60 to 65: 50 percent, work as long as possible, 10 percent; age 66 to 70: 9 percent; before age 60: 31 percent. SOURCE: KORN/FERRY INTERNATIONAL.

Back to Work

One-third of the surveyed retired senior executives returned to a full-time job within 18 months of retirement.

REASONS FOR RETURNING:	
Job satisfaction, enjoyment, or sense of accomplishment:	53%
Remain active or avoid boredom	29%
Contribution to society	18%
Where they returned:	
Employed by another organization	38%
Self-employed	32%
Free-lance or consultant	23%
Founded own company	7%

SOURCE: RUSSELL REYNOLDS ASSOCIATION, 1985.

Breakdown of the Workday

Amount of time we work to pay expenses in an 8-hour workday:

Federal and state taxes	2 hours, 45 minutes
Housing	1 hour, 25 minutes
Food and tobacco	57 minutes
Medical care	46 minutes
Transportation	39 minutes
Recreation	25 minutes
Other	1 hour, 3 minutes

SOURCE: THE TAX FOUNDATION, 1990.

A Ton of Laundry

The average family of 4 washes a ton of laundry each year.

SOURCE: PROCTER AND GAMBLE.

Ha, Ha, Ha

The average person laughs 15 times a day.

SOURCE: THE HUMOR PROJECT.

Wa, Wa, Wa

The average man cries 1.4 times a month. The average woman cries 5.3 times.

SOURCE: PROFESSOR WILLIAM FREY, DEPARTMENT OF PSYCHOLOGY, UNIVERSITY OF MINNESOTA, ST. PAUL.

Walking Speed

The average woman walks 256 feet per minute. The average man walks about 245.

SOURCE: PROFESSOR MICHAEL HILL, DEPARTMENT OF SOCIOLOGY, UNIVERSITY OF MINNESOTA, DULUTH.

Nightmares

The average adult has 1 nightmare a year.

SOURCE: DR. ERNEST HARTMANN, TUFTS UNIVERSITY MEDICAL SCHOOL.

Adoption Odds

Each year more than 1 million couples are seeking to adopt 30,000 white infants in the United States.

SOURCE: NATIONAL COMMITTEE FOR ADOPTION.

Bedtime

48 percent of men go to sleep between 10 and 11 P.M. as compared with only about 20 percent of women, who tend to stay up a little later.

SOURCE: MEL PORETZ AND BARRY SINROD. *THE FIRST REALLY IMPORTANT SURVEY OF AMERICAN HABITS.* PRICE, STERN, SLOAN, 1989.

Keeping in Touch

72 percent of females and 64 percent of males speak to their parents at least once a week. 51 percent of females and 54 percent of males speak to their spouse's parents at least once a week.

SOURCE: *SURVEY OF AMERICAN ADULTS.* KANE, PARSONS AND ASSOCIATES. *PARENTS MAGAZINE*, JUNE 1987.

Days of Our Lives

43 out of 100 Americans watch daytime television almost every day.

SOURCE: *AMERICA IN THE EIGHTIES,* R. H. BRUSKIN ASSOCIATES MARKET RESEARCH, 1985.

Getting in Shape

26 percent of women and 41 percent of men exercise strenuously 3 or more times a week.

SOURCE: *THE PREVENTION INDEX '87: A REPORT CARD ON THE NATION'S HEALTH.* A PROJECT OF *PREVENTION MAGAZINE.*

Feeling Stressed and Tense

22 percent of females and 16 percent of males feel stressed and tense at the end of almost every day.

SOURCE: *ROPER REPORTS*, JUNE 1989.

Sleeping Habits

Employed females sleep 55 hours a week. Employed males sleep 54 hours a week. Unemployed females sleep 57 hours a week. Unemployed males sleep 60 hours a week.

SOURCE: *AMERICAN DEMOGRAPHICS*, NOVEMBER 1989.

Americans Drive

The average American drives about 10,000 miles a year.

SOURCE: AMERICAN AUTOMOBILE ASSOCIATION.

Churchgoers

2 out of 5 Americans have attended church or synagogue in the last week. SOURCE: GEORGE GALLUP, JR. *THE GALLUP POLL; PUBLIC OPINION 1986.* SCHOLARLY RESOURCES, INC.

Daily Prayers

57 percent of Americans pray at least once a day.

SOURCE: GENERAL SOCIAL SURVEYS, 1972–1987. CONDUCTED FOR THE NATIONAL DATA PROGRAM FOR THE SOCIAL SCIENCES AT NATIONAL OPINION RESEARCH CENTER, UNIVERSITY OF CHICAGO.

Uninsured Mamas

Uninsured women spend an average of 1.9 days in the hospital for routine childbirth, whereas those with traditional insurance spend 2.3 days.

SOURCE: HEALTHCARE KNOWLEDGE SYSTEMS, ANN ARBOR, MICHIGAN.

Homeless Youth

There are about 500,000 runaways and "throwaways" yearly under the age of 18. During the summer of 1989 the number of homeless youths on any night was 68,000.

SOURCE: THE GENERAL ACCOUNTING OFFICE.

Trash Piles Up

Each month American households generate 28 pounds of newspaper, 17.2 pounds of glass containers, 6.8 pounds of tin cans, 4 pounds of cardboard, 1.9 pounds of aluminum cans, and .6 pounds of plastic.

SOURCE: BROWNING-FERRIS INDUSTRY.

What Happens to Our Garbage?

Each year Americans generate more than 150 million tons of garbage. 80 percent goes to landfills, 10 percent is incinerated, and only about 10 percent is recycled.

SOURCE: THE GARBAGE PROJECT, UNIVERSITY OF ARIZONA, TUCSON.

A Nation of Dropouts

27 percent of all U.S. high-school students, some 750,000 each year, drop out. In Japan the rate is 5 percent and in the Soviet Union the rate is 2 percent.

SOURCE: U.S. DEPARTMENT OF EDUCATION.

Older Women Have Fewer Babies

While 44 babies are born each year to every 10,000 women aged 40 to 44, only 2 are born to women aged 45 to 49.

SOURCE: *AMERICAN DEMOGRAPHICS*, JANUARY 1991.

The Way They Go

In 1986 to 1987, 85 percent of the dying chose to be buried and 14 percent chose cremation.

SOURCE: *FAMILY ECONOMICS REVIEW*, VOL. 2, NO. 4.

The Senior Boom

The elderly population increases rapidly in the United States.
1986: 12 percent of our population
2020: 21 percent of population (forecast)

SOURCE: FAMILY SERVICE AMERICA.

Age of CEOs

The typical CEO of America's largest companies takes power at the age of 51. Current chief executives average 56 years old.

SOURCE: *BUSINESS WEEK*, SEPTEMBER 25, 1989.

Age According to Race

	MEDIAN AGE	% UNDER 35	%35–64	%65 & OLDER
Hispanics	26.1	68%	27%	5%
Blacks	27.7	63%	28%	8%
Native Americans and Asians	29	61%	32%	7%
Whites	33.6	53%	34%	13%
Total population	—	54%	12%	—

SOURCE; CENSUS BUREAU ESTIMATES FOR 1989.

Sharing Space

In 1990, the worldwide number of time-share owners was 1.8 million.

SOURCE: AMERICAN RESORT AND RESIDENTIAL DEVELOPMENT ASSOCIATION.

Hard Times for Kids

Every day, 10 American children are killed by guns, 6 teenagers commit suicide, and 3,288 run away from home.

SOURCE: BARBARA REYNOLDS, "FROM THE HEART," *USA TODAY*, AUGUST 16, 1991.

Doctor Visits

Americans averaged 1.8 visits to the doctor in 1989. People in the age group of 15 to 24 averaged 1.9 visits, whereas senior citizens over age 75 averaged 5.9 visits.

SOURCE: NATIONAL AMBULATORY MEDICAL CARE SURVEY.

Youngest/Oldest States

YOUNGEST STATES	MEDIAN AGE	OLDEST STATES	MEDIAN AGE
1. Utah	25.7	1. Florida	36.4
2. Alaska	28.7	2. New Jersey	34.5
3. Wyoming	29.8	3. Connecticut	34.4
4. Louisiana	29.9	4. Pennsylvania	34.4
5. Mississippi	30	5. New York	33.8

SOURCE: STATE POPULATION AND HOUSEHOLD ESTIMATES, WITH AGE, SEX AND COMPONENTS OF CHANGE, 1981–1988. BUREAU OF THE CENSUS, CURRENT POPULATION REPORTS, SERIES P-25, NO. 1044.

Happily Married

The "very happily" married have sex 75 times a year; "not-too-happy" only about 43 times per year.

SOURCE: NATIONAL OPINION RESEARCH CENTER, UNIVERSITY OF CHICAGO.

Safe Days

3 out of 5 adult women don't know when they are most likely to become pregnant, and the figure is 4 out of 5 for teenage

girls. Pregnancy is most likely to occur when intercourse takes place 14 days after the first day of menstruation.

SOURCE: UNIVERSITY OF CALIFORNIA AT SAN FRANCISCO REPORT TITLED "ADOLESCENT PREGNANCY AND PARENTING IN CALIFORNIA."

Different Opinions About Time on the East and West coasts

In a 1991 poll, here are some interesting differences about what East Coasters and West Coasters think about time:

	EAST COAST	WEST COAST
There's not enough time for me to enjoy the money I earn . . .	20%	13%
I plan to slow down in the '90s . . .	33%	28%
I often feel under stress when I don't have enough time . . .	43%	30%
I feel trapped in daily routine . . .	26%	22%
I'd rather be kept busy than have a lot of time on my hands . . .	66%	59%
I would give up a day's pay to receive an extra day of free time . . .	54%	60%
At the end of the day, I often feel that I haven't accomplished what I set out to do . . .	34%	28%

SOURCE: HILTON HOTELS CORP.

More People Eat at McDonald's

In 1989, $7.29 of every $100 spent eating and drinking outside of the home in the United States was spent at McDonald's. 1 in every 4 Americans who eat breakfast away from home in the United States is served at McDonald's.

SOURCE: MCDONALD'S CORPORATION.

Three Cups a Day

100 million Americans drink 3 cups of coffee a day.

SOURCE: "TODAY," SEPTEMBER 4, 1991.

Keeping Checkbook in Check

How often do you bring your checkbook balance up to date? Here is what others do.

	MEN	WOMEN	TOTAL AVERAGE
Every time a check is written	37%	42%	40%
Once a week	18%	14%	16%
Less often than once a week	30%	24%	27%
Never	12%	16%	14%

NOTE: Figures do not add up to 100 percent because some respondents either did not know the answer to the question or did not answer.

SOURCE: THE GALLUP ORGANIZATION FOR VISA USA, FROM *GOOD HOUSEKEEPING*, OCTOBER 1991.

What Americans Throw Away

According to the Environmental Protection Agency, here is what was dumped into landfills by volume in 1988.

ITEM	% OF TOTAL	MILLION TONS
Newspapers, books, magazines	8.4	13.5
Corrugated boxes	8.4	12.6
Other paper	17.2	27.4
Disposable diapers	3.3	2.7
Durable goods (furniture, appliances, etc.)	8.0	5.7
Plastics	8.6	5.9
Metals and glass	14.1	23.7
Yard waste	10.3	31.0

ITEM	% OF TOTAL	MILLION TONS
Food waste	3.3	13.2
Miscellaneous (rubber textiles, wood, etc.)	18.4	20.3

SOURCE: ENVIRONMENTAL PROTECTION AGENCY, 1990 REPORT.

Rice Eaters

One-half of the people in the world eat rice every single day.

SOURCE: USA RICE COUNCIL.

Late Summer Brides

More couples get married in late summer than in the traditional month of June. 20 percent of all weddings are celebrated in August and September, compared with only 12 percent in June.

SOURCE: *BRIDE'S* MAGAZINE.

American Leisure Time as Compared to Japanese Leisure Time

A 1991 study titled *At Our Leisure*, reveals that American men and women work slightly more hours a week than do Japanese men and women, contradicting a popular belief. Apparently, because their commuting times are considerably longer on the average, Japanese have slightly less time for leisure—about 40 hours a week to Americans' 41 hours. One-third of Americans' leisure time is spent watching television. SOURCE: RESEARCH ALERT.

How Americans Spend Their Leisure Time

More than 75 percent of U.S. households include somebody involved in a hobby. Needlepoint, sewing, and knitting top the list, according to a 1991 study titled *At Our Leisure*. Other popular activities include cake decorating, candy making, and drawing. Some 71 percent of American adults gamble; 58 percent say they lose more than they win. Some 54 percent say that they have bought lottery tickets.

SOURCE: IBID.

5. Time and the Workplace

The Average Work Week

The average work week including commuting is about 47 hours.

SOURCE: LOUIS HARRIS ASSOCIATES.

Wasted Time for Executives

The average executive spends 15 minutes a day on hold (60 hours a year), 32 minutes per day reading or writing unnecessary memos (128 hours per year), and 72 minutes per day at unnecessary meetings (288 hours, or more than 7 weeks per year).

SOURCE: ACCOUNTEMPS, A PERSONNEL AGENCY'S SURVEY OF 200 EXECUTIVES.

Finding a New Job

The average time to find a new job was 5.9 months in 1989.

SOURCE: DRAKE BEAM MORIN.

Telemarketing Calls

75,000 stockbrokers made 1.5 billion telemarketing calls in 1990. In addition, about 300,000 telemarketing agents make some 18 million calls a day.

SOURCE: AMERICAN TELEMARKETING ASSOCIATION, *TELEMARKETING MAGAZINE*.

Working for Same Employer

Almost half the workers age 45 to 54 have been with their current employer for 10 years or more, compared with a median of 6 years for workers aged 35 to 44.

SOURCE: CENSUS BUREAU.

Without a Job

In 1989, just half of the unemployed were without a job for 5 or more weeks. But about 70 percent of workers 45 to 64 were without a job for 5 weeks or more.

SOURCE: BUREAU OF LABOR STATISTICS, 1989.

Growth of Home-Based Businesses

In 1980 there were about 5.7 million home-based businesses compared with about 14.6 million full-time home-based businesses in 1989.

SOURCE: AMERICAN HOME BUSINESS ASSOCIATION.

PCs at Home

In 1988, 8 percent of personal computer owners spent 1 hour or less each week on their personal computer at home; 17 percent spent 2 to 3 hours; 9 percent spent 4 to 5 hours; 6 percent spent 6 to 8 hours; 3 percent spent 8 to 9 hours; 8 percent spent 10 hours; and 29 percent of personal computer owners spent 11 hours or more each week on their computers at home.

SOURCE: ELECTRONIC INDUSTRIES ASSOCIATION.

Wives Work More

Combining housework and outside employment, including commuting time, wives work 71 hours per week. Husbands work 55 hours per week. Females who work full time spend an average of 25 hours a week working around the house. Males who work full time spend 13 hours.

SOURCE: TOM AND NANCY BIRACREE. *ALMANAC OF THE AMERICAN PEOPLE.* FACTS ON FILE, 1988.

Working Full Time

68 percent of females work full time compared with 86 percent of males. 49 percent of females work full time year round compared with 67 percent of males. SOURCE: IBID.

Short-Lived Jobs

52 percent of females and 35 percent of males have worked less than 5 years at the jobs they held the longest.

SOURCE: *VITAL AND HEALTH STATISTICS: HEALTH CHARACTERISTICS BY OCCUPATION AND INDUSTRY OF LONGEST EMPLOYMENT*. NATIONAL CENTER FOR HEALTH STATISTICS, JUNE 1989.

Long-Lived Jobs

8 percent of females and 21 percent of males have worked at least 20 years at the jobs they held the longest. SOURCE: IBID.

Men Work More Years Than Women

By the age of 64, women are away from their work an average of 14.7 years. Men are away an average of 1.6 years.

SOURCE: *MALE-FEMALE DIFFERENCES IN WORK EXPERIENCE, OCCUPATION, AND EARNINGS: 1984*. CURRENT POPULATION REPORTS. BUREAU OF THE CENSUS, 1987.

Paid Vacation Days

The average American worker gets 8.7 paid vacation days a year. SOURCE: U.S. BUREAU OF LABOR STATISTICS.

Walking While Working

The average factory worker walks about 2,227 miles a year on the job. The average housewife averages about 1,037.

SOURCE: SCHOLL, INC.

Lost Work Hours Due to Alcoholism

The United States loses an estimated 6 million hours of work each year due to alcoholism.

SOURCE: RESEARCH TRIANGLE INSTITUTE, RESEARCH TRIANGLE PARK, NC.

Part-Timers

The average part-time job is 21 hours a week.

SOURCE: MIKE FEINSILBER AND WILLIAM B. MEAD. *AMERICAN AVERAGES*. DOUBLEDAY, 1980.

300 Lays a Day

The average bricklayer lays about 300 bricks a day.

SOURCE: IBID.

Barbers vs. Stylists

The average barber gives 12 to 17 haircuts a day, shearing each customer in about 15 minutes. The average hairstylist fixes up to 12 customers a day, averaging about 30 to 45 minutes each.

SOURCE: ASSOCIATED MASTER BARBERS AND BEAUTICIANS OF AMERICA.

Car Pooling

1 out of 5 Americans car pools to work.

SOURCE: 1980 CENSUS OF POPULATION: GENERAL SOCIAL AND ECONOMIC CHARACTERISTICS, UNITED STATES SUMMARY. BUREAU OF THE CENSUS. U.S. DEPARTMENT OF COMMERCE, 1983.

Excuse Me!

The average manager is interrupted every 8 minutes. 50 percent are interrupted 8 or 9 times an hour, 22 percent 10 to 11 times, 11 percent 6 to 7 times, 10 percent 4 to 5 times, 5 percent 1 to 3 times, and 2 percent more than 12 times.

SOURCE: PRIORITY MANAGEMENT SYSTEMS, INC.

New Franchises

Every 17 minutes a new franchise opens in the United States. SOURCE: INTERNATIONAL FRANCHISE ASSOCIATION.

A Mailman's Day

U.S. letter carriers work 8-hour days and take a half hour for lunch. They spend approximately 47 percent of their 8-hour day in the office and the remaining 53 percent on the street.

SOURCE: NATIONAL ASSOCIATION OF LETTER CARRIERS.

Part-Time Jobs Pay Less

Part-timers receive about 60 cents an hour to every dollar paid full-timers. Part-timers are also less likely to get health benefits.

SOURCE: CENTER FOR SOCIAL POLICY STUDIES, GEORGE WASHINGTON UNIVERSITY.

The 25 Hottest County Economies

Projected new jobs, in thousands, by county, 1989 to 2000:

COUNTY	NEW JOBS IN THOUSANDS
1. Orange, California	674
2. Los Angeles, California	652
3. Harris, Texas	452
4. Maricopa, Arizona	434
5. San Diego, California	420
6. Dallas, Texas	371
7. Santa Clara, California	304
8. Fairfax/Fairfax City/ Falls Church, Virginia	258
9. King, Washington	253
10. Broward, Florida	246
11. Palm Beach, Florida	215
12. Dade, Florida	199
13. Oakland, Michigan	193
14. Suffolk, New York	192

COUNTY	NEW JOBS IN THOUSANDS
15. Du Page, Illinois	180
16. St. Louis, Missouri	160
17. Tarrant, Texas	159
18. Bexar, Texas	153
19. Hennepin, Minnesota	153
20. Middlesex, Massachusetts	151
21. Sacramento, California	151
22. Arapahoe, Colorado	146
23. Cob, Georgia	146
24. Gwinnett, Georgia	145
25. Hillsborough, Florida	144

SOURCE: NPA DATA SERVICES, INC. IN *AMERICAN DEMOGRAPHICS*, JANUARY 1991.

Let Your Fingers Do the Walking

Every day, a computer operator moves his or her fingers an incredible 90,000 or more times in the same direction (based on 50-words-per-minute typing at 6 hours per day).

SOURCE: EROGONOMICS, INC.

Membership in Unions on the Decline

YEAR	EMPLOYED WORKERS IN UNIONS (MILLIONS)	% OF NATION'S WORK FORCE
1980	20.1	23.0
1983	17.7	20.1
1984	17.3	18.8
1985	17.0	18.0
1986	16.9	17.5
1987	16.9	17.0
1988	17.0	16.8
1989	16.9	16.4
1990	16.7	16.1

SOURCE: BUREAU OF LABOR STATISTICS, U.S. DEPARTMENT OF LABOR, 1991.

Today's Professional Women

111,000 or 19 percent of physicians in the United States are female. 151,000, or 21 percent of the lawyers are female, and 730,000 women are accountants, which, for the first time, exceeded 50 percent in 1990. 42.5 percent of law students in the United States are female.

SOURCE: U.S. DEPARTMENT OF LABOR, WOMEN'S BUREAU, 1991.

The Work That Women Do

Here is a list of the 10 most common jobs that working women held during the past 100 years.

1890	1940	1990
1. Servant	1. Servant	1. Secretary
2. Agricultural laborer	2. Stenographer, secretary	2. Cashier
3. Dressmaker	3. Teacher	3. Bookkeeper
4. Teacher	4. Clerical worker	4. Registered nurse
5. Farmer, planter	5. Sales worker	5. Nursing aid orderly
6. Laundress	6. Factory worker (apparel)	6. Elementary teacher
7. Seamstress	7. Bookkeeper, accountant, cashier	7. Waitress
8. Cotton-mill operative	8. Waitress	8. Sales worker
9. Housekeeper, steward	9. Housekeeper	9. Child care
10. Clerk, cashier	10. Nurse	10. Cook

SOURCE: IBID.

Commuter Miles to Work in United States

The distance traveled for commuting to work in the United States averaged 10.6 miles in 1990, up from 8.6 miles in 1983.

SOURCE: IBID.

The Advantage of Being Self-Employed

Owners of small businesses work an average of 52.5 hours a week as compared to 43.5 hours for those people in the general work force. SOURCE: NATIONAL ASSOCIATION FOR THE SELF-EMPLOYED.

Paid Holidays

The average U.S. employer spends $820 per employee on holiday benefits each year. SOURCE: U.S. CHAMBER OF COMMERCE.

Working Can Be Dangerous to Your Health

There were 6.8 million on-the-job injuries and illnesses in 1990. Nearly 9 of every 100 workers got sick or injured because of their job. Nearly half of the 1990 cases were serious enough to require workers to lose job time or have their work activity restricted. Disorders associated with repeated trauma, such as carpal tunnel syndrome, comprised almost 60 percent of all illnesses. These disorders are often suffered by typists or assembly-line workers who repeat the same action throughout the day. SOURCE: BUREAU OF LABOR STATISTICS.

6. Health and Accidents

Diabetes

Each day 1,500 people will be told they have diabetes; 20 percent of all Americans over the age of 55 are diabetics.

SOURCE: AMERICAN DIABETES ASSOCIATION.

Cancer Survival Rates

An estimated 50 percent of all people who contract cancer will be alive 5 years after they are diagnosed.

SOURCE: AMERICAN CANCER SOCIETY.

AIDS Testing

2 percent of females and 5 percent of males had their blood tested for AIDS in 1988. SOURCE: *ROPER REPORTS*, FEBRUARY 1989.

Heart Murmurs

6 out of 25 Americans with heart murmurs are under 18 years of age. SOURCE: CURRENT ESTIMATES FROM THE NATIONAL HEALTH INTERVIEW SURVEY. VITAL AND HEALTH STATISTICS. PUBLIC HEALTH SERVICE. U.S. DEPARTMENT OF HEALTH AND HUMAN SERVICES, 1987.

Death by Heart Disease

Heart disease claims nearly 1 million lives each year in America.

SOURCE: THE UNITED WAY.

Heart Attacks Are Greater Threat to Women

Women who have heart attacks are twice as likely to die within the first few weeks than men. 39 percent of women die within a year after a heart attack compared with 31 percent for men.

SOURCE: AMERICAN HEART ASSOCIATION.

Even Greater Threat to Black Women

From ages 35 to 74, the death rate from heart attack among black women is 1½ times that of white women and 3 times that of women of other races. After age 75, death rates for white women are higher.

SOURCE: IBID.

AIDS Cases Double

It takes an average of about 12 months for the number of AIDS cases to double.

SOURCE: CENTERS FOR DISEASE CONTROL, ATLANTA.

Brush Your Teeth

While dentists recommend brushing your teeth 3 times daily, only 20 percent of Americans actually do. 56 percent brush their teeth 2 times a day, and 19 percent only once a day. Who knows what the other 5 percent do!

SOURCE: GALLUP SURVEY OF 1,200 PEOPLE FOR AMERICAN DENTAL ASSOCIATION.

Health Care Costs

The United States spends almost $1.5 billion a day on health care. In 1987, the United States spent $500 billion on health care, nearly 12 percent of the U.S. GNP.

SOURCE: NATIONAL LEADERSHIP COMMISSION ON HEALTH CARE, 1989.

The Cost of Medical/Dental Insurance

The average cost of medical/dental plans in the United States was $2,748 in 1989.

SOURCE: A FOSTER HIGGINS & CO. INC. SURVEY OF 1,943 EMPLOYEES.

Infant Mortality Rate

Each year 40,000 babies die before their first birthday, for a national average of 9.9 deaths per 1,000 births. Underdeveloped nations have a death rate of 99 deaths per 1,000 babies.

SOURCE: THE NATIONAL CENTER FOR HEALTH STATISTICS.

Children with AIDS

60 to 70 percent of children with AIDS die within 2 years of diagnosis. For every child who is diagnosed with the HIV virus, health experts estimate that another 2 to 10 children are actually infected with the virus.

SOURCE: CENTERS FOR DISEASE CONTROL, ATLANTA.

Girl Babies Will Outlive Boy Babies

Girls born in 1989 can expect to live 78.6 years as compared with 71.8 for boys. This averages 75.2 years for both sexes.

SOURCE: METROPOLITAN LIFE.

Birth Spacing

When there is less than 2 years between births, the risk of the second child dying in infancy is increased between 60 and 70 percent. The odds also double that the earlier child will die before age 5.
SOURCE: POPULATION CRISIS COMMITTEE.

Older Moms

7 percent of the pregnancies are among women older than 35 at delivery.

SOURCE: MARK LANDON OF THE OHIO STATE UNIVERSITY, COLUMBUS.

Spontaneous Abortions Increase with Age

The odds of spontaneous abortions rise with age. They are 12 to 15 percent for a woman in her early twenties as compared with 25 percent for a woman age 40.

SOURCE: DR. JOE LEIGH SIMPSON, CHAIRMAN OF OBSTETRICS AND GYNECOLOGY, UNIVERSITY OF TENNESSEE SCHOOL OF MEDICINE, MEMPHIS.

The Reproductive Cycle

Most women have a 28-day reproductive cycle, with ovulation occurring about 14 days before the first day of the next menstrual cycle. But, the one day of each cycle on which ovulation occurs may vary. Although each cycle's egg remains viable for only a few hours, sperm can live up to 8 days in a woman's reproductive tract, so intercourse a few days before ovulation, or on the day of ovulation, may lead to conception.

SOURCE: THE KINSEY REPORT.

AIDS—An Expensive Disease

The total medical cost of an AIDS patient in his thirties is between $70,000 and $141,000. That is much higher than the cost of treating someone in his thirties who has a heart attack ($67,000), digestive cancer ($47,000), or leukemia ($29,000). In the 1990s treating AIDS will cost tens of billions of dollars each year. SOURCE: RAND CORPORATION.

There's a Virus Going Around

10 percent of the U.S. population is affected by influenza each year. SOURCE: HOFFMAN-LA ROCHE FLU TRACK CENTER.

Abortion Safer than Having a Baby

Having an abortion is 7 to 25 times safer than carrying a fetus to term for 9 months and does not increase a woman's subsequent risk of infertility or miscarriage.

SOURCE: U.S. DEPARTMENT OF HEALTH AND HUMAN SERVICES.

Average Hospital Stay

According to a 1989 survey, the average patient stays in a community hospital in the United States for 7.2 days.

SOURCE: AMERICAN HOSPITAL ASSOCIATION. *HOSPITAL STATISTICS 1990–1991.*

Visiting the Hospital

15 percent of females and 10 percent of males age 17 and older enter the hospital each year.

SOURCE: *VITAL AND HEALTH STATISTICS: HEALTH CHARACTERISTICS BY OCCUPATION AND INDUSTRY OF LONGEST EMPLOYMENT.* NATIONAL CENTER FOR HEALTH STATISTICS, JUNE 1989.

Doc-Shy

1 out of 25 Americans hasn't seen a doctor in at least 5 years.

SOURCE: CURRENT ESTIMATES FROM THE NATIONAL HEALTH INTERVIEW SURVEY—VITAL AND HEALTH STATISTICS. PUBLIC HEALTH SERVICE. U.S. DEPARTMENT OF HEALTH AND HUMAN SERVICES, 1987.

Visiting the Doctor

81 percent of females and 67 percent of males visit a physician each year. SOURCE: *VITAL AND HEALTH STATISTICS: HEALTH CHARACTERISTICS BY OCCUPATION AND INDUSTRY OF LONGEST EMPLOYMENT.* NATIONAL CENTER FOR HEALTH STATISTICS, JUNE 1989.

Pregnancy Risks According to Age

MATERNAL AGE	RISK OF DOWN'S SYNDROME	TOTAL RISK FOR CHROMOSOME ABNORMALITIES
20	1 in 1,667	1 in 526
22	1 in 1,429	1 in 500
24	1 in 1,250	1 in 476
26	1 in 1,176	1 in 476
28	1 in 1,053	1 in 435
30	1 in 952	1 in 384
32	1 in 796	1 in 322
34	1 in 500	1 in 260
36	1 in 294	1 in 164
38	1 in 175	1 in 103
40	1 in 106	1 in 65
42	1 in 64	1 in 40
44	1 in 38	1 in 25

SOURCE: *AMERICAN JOURNAL OF OBSTETRICS AND GYNECOLOGY,* 1989.

Babies Born Every Hour to Teenagers

56 babies are born to teenage mothers every hour in the United States. SOURCE: NATIONAL CENTER FOR HEALTH STATISTICS.

Jerry's Kids

More than 37 million Americans over 15 years old suffer some functional physical limitation and 13.5 percent more are severely limited. SOURCE: THE UNITED WAY.

The Older You Are, the Longer You'll Live

Americans who celebrate their seventy-fifth birthday have an average life expectancy of 85.9 years. SOURCE: METROPOLITAN LIFE.

Your Smoking Is Dangerous to Your Children's Health

50 percent of American preschoolers were exposed to cigarette smoke in their households in 1988. Children under the age of 6 who have been exposed to smoke have higher rates of fair or poor health. SOURCE: U.S. DEPARTMENT OF HEALTH.

Women Who Smoke Get Ulcers

1 out of every 10 women who smoke can expect to develop a stomach ulcer within the next 12 years. Those women who kick the habit can reduce their risk of ulcers to nearly that of women who have never smoked. The risk is the greatest among women who smoke a pack or more of cigarettes a day.

SOURCE: *ARCHIVES OF INTERNAL MEDICINE.*

Smoking Is Bad for a Woman's Heart

Women smokers have a 3.6 times greater risk of a heart attack compared with women who have never smoked. However, the risk is the same if the smoker quits for 3 or more years.

SOURCE: *NEW ENGLAND JOURNAL OF MEDICINE.*

Heavy Smokers Can't Smell

Two-or-more-packs-a-day smokers lose 15 to 20 percent of their sense of smell. It takes 10 years for the presmoking sense of smell to return.

SOURCE: UNIVERSITY OF PENNSYLVANIA SCHOOL OF MEDICINE.

Don't Try It, You Might Like It

37 percent of the population age 12 and over have tried marijuana, cocaine, and other illicit drugs in their lifetime. 14 percent have used these substances at least once in the last month. 75 percent of the American population has tried cigarettes and 29 percent are current smokers.

SOURCE: NATIONAL INSTITUTE ON DRUG ABUSE.

How Long Drugs Stay in Urine

Nicotine	24 to 48 hours
Marijuana	10 to 35 days
Cocaine	24 to 36 hours
Amphetamines	48 to 72 hours
PCP	48 to 78 hours
Valium et al.	48 to 76 hours
Phenylpropanolamine	24 to 48 hours
Heroin	48 to 72 hours

SOURCE: THE NATIONAL PARENTS' RESOURCE INSTITUTE FOR DRUG EDUCATION, INC. (PRIDE).

Death by Suicide

An average of 1 person every 17.1 minutes kills themselves. Each year, more than 30,000 Americans commit suicide.

SOURCE: AMERICAN ASSOCIATION OF SUICIDOLOGY.

Too Much Meat

Americans consumed an average of 218.4 pounds of meat per person in 1989—in excess of a half-pound of meat each day.

SOURCE: AMERICAN DIETETIC ASSOCIATION.

Health Huckstering in the United States

Americans are being ripped off by health quackery by an

estimated $40 billion a year. False promises to retard or reverse aging and prevent, treat, or cure almost any malady from athlete's foot to cancer are big business in the United States. The vast majority of these products claim to cure or relieve diseases associated with aging, and as much as 60 percent of the proceeds from quack products may come from America's elderly. Two-thirds of that revenue involves products represented as "nutritional."

SOURCE; WILLIAM BARNHILL, "PULLING THE PLUG ON THE QUACKS," *AARP BULLETIN*, JULY–AUGUST 1991, P. 2.

Dentist Visits

52 percent of females and 48 percent of males visit a dentist each year. SOURCE: *VITAL AND HEALTH STATISTICS: HEALTH CHARACTERISTICS BY OCCUPATION AND INDUSTRY OF LONGEST EMPLOYMENT*. NATIONAL CENTER FOR HEALTH STATISTICS, JUNE 1989.

Annual Operations

Each year 11 percent of females and 8 percent of males have operations. SOURCE; TOM AND NANCY BIRACREE. *ALMANAC OF THE AMERICAN PEOPLE*. FACTS ON FILE, 1988.

Short-Stay Hospitals

The average length of stay for male patients at short-stay hospitals is 7.1 days and 6.2 days for females.

SOURCE: NATIONAL CENTER FOR HEALTH STATISTICS, UTILIZATION OF SHORT-STAY HOSPITALS, 1988.

Discharged Seniors

Every day in the United States 31,991 seniors are discharged from hospitals after staying an average of 9 days. That is 8 days for persons age 65 to 74 and 9 days for persons over the age of 75. SOURCE: IBID.

Seniors Contact Physicians

Every day in the United States 778,000 seniors call or visit a physician. The average senior makes about 9 contacts a year with his or her physician.

SOURCE: NATIONAL CENTER FOR HEALTH STATISTICS, CURRENT ESTIMATES, 1988, 1989.

Lonely Seniors Visit Doctor More

Seniors living alone visit the doctor an average of 7 times per year compared with 4.5 times for those living with others.

SOURCE: OLDER AMERICANS REPORTS, APRIL 15, 1988.

Fast Turnover of Patients in Doctor's Office

45 percent of visits to doctors' offices last less than 11 minutes.

SOURCE: NATIONAL CENTER FOR HEALTH STATISTICS, HYATTSVILLE, MD.

Lonely Seniors in Bed Less

Sick seniors who live alone spend an average of 11 days in bed each year compared with 19 days for those living with others.

SOURCE: OLDER AMERICANS REPORTS, APRIL 15, 1988.

Funds to the Dying

28 percent of Medicare funds go to people with less than 1 year to live.

SOURCE: HEALTH CARE FINANCING ADMINISTRATION, BALTIMORE, MD.

Daily Calories

Females age 19 to 50 eat food supplying an average of 1,661 calories a day. Males age 19 to 50 average 2,560 calories a day.

SOURCE: U.S. DEPARTMENT OF AGRICULTURE.

Beginning a Diet

65 percent of females and 25 percent of males begin at least 1 diet a year.

SOURCE: TOM AND NANCY BIRACREE. *ALMANAC OF THE AMERICAN PEOPLE*. FACTS ON FILE, 1988.

Millions Diet Each Day

On an average day 60 million females and 41 million males are on a diet. SOURCE: TOM HEYMANN. *ON AN AVERAGE DAY*. FAWCETT, 1989.

Exercising Regularly

Two-thirds of the U.S. population exercise on a regular basis (more than once per week). 3 out of 10 adults exercise 5 or more times per week.

SOURCE: BOOTH RESEARCH SERVICES, INC., ATLANTA, GA.

Dieting Attempts and Results

Dieters who began their current diet less than 1 year ago averaged 3 different dieting attempts during 1990. Among all dieters, nearly half (47 percent) have been on their current diet for less than 6 months. Among dieters trying to reduce, 87 percent said they lost weight (an average of 13 pounds) on their current diet. SOURCE: 1991 CALORIE CONTROL COUNCIL SURVEY.

Expending Calories

Expenditure in calories by a 150-pound person:

ACTIVITY	TOTAL CALORIES USED PER HOUR
Ballroom dancing	125–310
Walking slowly (2½ mph)	210–230
Brisk walking (4 mph)	250–345
Cycling	315–480
Jogging	315–480

ACTIVITY	TOTAL CALORIES USED PER HOUR
Tennis	315–480
Aerobic dancing	480–625
Basketball	480–625
Cross-country skiing	480–625
Swimming	480–625

SOURCE: USDA/USDHHS DIETARY GUIDELINES FOR AMERICANS.

Crack Babies

Annually, an estimated 375,000 infants are exposed to health-threatening drugs because 1 in 10 mothers takes illegal drugs during pregnancy. It costs $100,000 to care for a crack-addicted infant during the first 3 months of its life. SOURCE: THE UNITED WAY.

Taking Legal Drugs

44 percent of females and 18 percent of males took a prescription drug during the past week. 56 percent of females and 47 percent of males took a nonprescription drug in the past week. SOURCE: *ROPER REPORTS*, JUNE 1989.

First Mammograms

Major cancer organizations recommend that a woman have her first mammogram between the ages of 35 and 40.

SOURCE; KINSEY INSTITUTE FOR RESEARCH IN SEX, GENDER AND REPRODUCTION.

Narcolepsy Attacks

These sleeping-disorder victims often have "sleep attacks" during the day, which usually last for less than 30 minutes.

SOURCE; U.S. DEPARTMENT OF HEALTH AND HUMAN SERVICES.

Diagnosis for Narcoleptics

The average person who is diagnosed as suffering from narcolepsy has lived with the symptoms for 10 to 15 years and has sought help from 3 to 5 doctors prior to the initial correct diagnosis. SOURCE: THE AMERICAN NARCOLEPSY ASSOCIATION.

Workdays Lost Because of Headaches

It is estimated that U.S. industry has lost $50 billion per year due to absenteeism and medical expenses caused by headache, and migraine sufferers lost more than 157 million workdays each year. SOURCE: NATIONAL HEADACHE FOUNDATION.

Migraine Sufferers

Migraine sufferers have headaches that last anywhere from a few hours to a number of days. Most sufferers experience between 1 and 4 attacks per month SOURCE: IBID.

Tips for Living Longer

For the average man who turned 35 last year, getting blood pressure under control will add 1 year of life. Getting cholesterol under 200 increased longevity by 8 months. Eliminating smoking adds 10 months and losing weight adds 7 months.

For a woman, blood pressure control adds 5 months of life, cholesterol lowering adds 10 months, smoking cessation 8 months, and weight loss 5 months.

SOURCE: *CIRCULATION*, APRIL 1991.

Harmful Rays

In 1991, about 28,000 Americans developed malignant melanoma, a sun-related skin cancer that often occurs in or near moles; 6,000 people died from it.

SOURCE: DARRELL S. RIGEL, M.D., NEW YORK UNIVERSITY.

Yesteryear's Sunburn

There is a delay of 10 to 20 years from the time when damage from the sun occurs until melanoma develops and can be detected. SOURCE: IBID.

Most Operations

Dr. M. C. Modi, an eye surgeon in India, has performed as many as 833 cataract operations in a single day for a career total of 564,834 through January 1987.

SOURCE: GUINNESS BOOK OF WORLD RECORDS, 1990.

Longest Operation

Mrs. Gertrude Levandowski had a cyst removed that reduced her weight by 308 pounds. The surgery took a total of 96 hours because the patient suffered from a weak heart and the surgeons had to exercise the utmost caution. SOURCE: IBID.

Longest Stay in Mental Hospital

After spending more than 99 years in mental institutions, Miss Martha Nelson died in January 1975 at age 103, in the Orient State Institution, Ohio. SOURCE: IBID.

Iron Lung Survival

Mrs. Laurel Nisbet was in an iron lung continuously from June 25, 1948, to her death on August 22, 1985, surviving a total of 37 years, 58 days. SOURCE: IBID.

Longest Coma

Elaine Esposito went into a coma after an appendectomy at age 6. She died on November 25, 1978, age 43 years, 357 days, having remained in a coma for 37 years, 111 days.

SOURCE: IBID.

Heart Stoppage

Jan Egil Refsdahl, a Norwegian fisherman who fell overboard in the icy waters off Bergen on December 7, 1987, was rushed to a nearby hospital after his body temperature fell to 77 degrees and his heart stopped beating. After 4 hours of heart stoppage, he made a full recovery when he was connected to a heart-lung machine normally used for heart surgery.

SOURCE: IBID.

Longest Surviving Heart Transplantee

Emmanuel Vitria of Marseilles, France, received a heart transplant from Pierre Ponson, 20, on November 27, 1968, and lived until May 9, 1987. SOURCE: IBID.

Longest Fast

The longest period during which anyone has gone without solid food is 382 days. It was done by Angus Barbieri of Tayport, Fife, Scotland, who lived on tea, coffee, water, soda water, and vitamins from June 1965 to July 1966 in Maryfield Hospital, Dundee, Angus, Scotland. His weight dropped from 472 pounds to 178 pounds. SOURCE: IBID.

Chronic Sneezing

Donna Griffiths started sneezing on January 13, 1981, and continued sneezing until September 16, 1983, the 978th day.

SOURCE: IBID.

Donating Blood

5 percent of all Americans give blood at least once a year. Of those who do, 80 percent are repeat donors.

SOURCE: AMERICAN RED CROSS GALLUP POLL.

Pass the Blood, Bub

Approximately 2 percent of Americans were transfused in the past year. In every minute of the day, 23 units of blood or red blood cells are transfused. SOURCE: THE AMERICAN RED CROSS.

Vet Bills

Americans spend more than $5 billion a year at the vet, or at least $25 per animal. SOURCE: KAREN GAVZER, MARKETING DIRECTOR OF THE AMERICAN VETERINARY MEDICAL ASSOCIATION.

Nose Jobs

In 1988, 186,032 people got plastic surgery on their noses.
SOURCE: AMERICAN ACADEMY OF FACIAL PLASTIC AND RECONSTRUCTIVE SURGERY.

Cosmetic Surgery

TYPE	LENGTH OF SURGERY	RECOVERY TIME
Liposuction	1–2 hours	Normal appearance: up to 12 weeks for all swelling/bruising to subside. Feeling better: 1–3 weeks.
Breast lift	1½–3½ hours	Normal appearance: up to 6 weeks for all swelling to subside, and up to 6–12 months for scars to fade. Feeling better: 2–4 weeks.
Tummy tuck	2–5 hours	Normal appearance: 3–6 weeks (up to 2 years for scar to fade and flatten). Feeling better: 3–6 weeks.
Neck/face-lift	2–5 hours	Normal appearance: 10 days to 3 weeks. Feeling better: 1–2 weeks.
Forehead lift	1–2 hours	Normal appearance: 10 days to 3 weeks. Feeling better: 1–2 weeks.
Eyelid surgery	1–2 hours	Normal appearance: 5–14 days. Feeling better: 5 days to 2 weeks.

TYPE	LENGTH OF SURGERY	RECOVERY TIME
Ear pinning	1–2 hours	Normal appearance: 1 week. Feeling better: 1 week.
Nose surgery	1–2 hours	Normal appearance: 1–2 weeks. (All swelling may not disappear for a year or longer.) Feeling better: 1 to 2 weeks.
Cheek augmentation	1 hour	Normal appearance: 1–2 weeks. Feeling better: 7–10 days.
Chin augmentation	30 minutes–2 hours	Normal appearance: 2–3 weeks. Feeling better: 1–3 weeks.
Chemical peel	15 minutes–1 hour.	Normal appearance: 3–4 weeks. Feeling better: 7–14 days.
Dermabrasion	30 minutes–2 hours. (More than 1 session may be needed for deep scars.)	Normal appearance: 3–4 weeks. Feeling better: 3–14 days.
Collagen or fat injections	15–20 minutes per session	Normal appearance: up to 10 days. Feeling better: 1 day.
Hair replacement	1–3 hours per session (usually more than 1 session is needed)	Normal appearance: 5–14 days. Feeling better: 1–5 days.
Breast enlargement	1–2 hours	Normal appearance: up to 6 weeks for all swelling to subside, and up to 6–12 months for scars to fade. Feeling better: 2–4 weeks.
Breast reduction	2–5 hours	Normal appearance: up to 6 weeks for all swelling/bruising to disappear, and up to 1 year for scars to fade and flatten. Feeling better: 2–3 weeks.

SOURCE: AMERICAN SOCIETY OF PLASTIC AND RECONSTRUCTIVE SURGEONS, INC.

Motor Vehicle Deaths

In 1989, 46,900 people died in motor vehicle accidents. This is about 1 death every 11 minutes by a motor vehicle accident.

SOURCES: NATIONAL SAFETY COUNCIL AND AUTHORS' CALCULATIONS.

Death by Falls

In 1989, 12,400 people died from falls. This averages about 1 death every 42 minutes. SOURCE: IBID.

Drowning Deaths

In 1989, 4,600 people drowned. This averages 1 person about every 2 hours. SOURCE: IBID.

Burning to Death

In 1989, 4,400 people burned to death. This averages about 1 person every 2 hours. SOURCE: IBID.

Choking to Death

In 1989, 3,900 people died from ingesting food or an object. This averages about 1 person every 2 hours, 14 minutes.

SOURCE: IBID.

Poisoned to Death

In 1989, 5,600 people were poisoned to death, either by drinking or eating a poisonous substance. This averages about 1 death every hour and a half. An additional 900 people died from poison by gas. SOURCE: IBID.

Airline Accidents

In 1989 there were 24 accidents on large airlines in the United States; 8 of them were fatal. In these 8 accidents, 131 people died. SOURCE: NATIONAL SAFETY COUNCIL.

Time Lost Because of Accidents

In 1988, 35 million days were lost in the workplace due to accidents. SOURCE: *ACCIDENT FACTS*, 1989 EDITION.

School Bus Accidents

110 persons nationwide were killed during the 1987 to 1988 school year, including 40 pupils, 5 bus drivers, and 65 other persons. SOURCE: IBID.

Deaths from Fires

Cigarettes were associated with 29 percent of the 4,470 civilian fire deaths in 1989. The next most frequent causes of fire deaths were heating equipment (13 percent) and electrical distribution (12 percent). SOURCE: U.S. CONSUMER PRODUCT SAFETY COMMISSION/ EPHA, FROM DATA OBTAINED FROM THE USFA AND NFPA.

Fire Fatalities

Every year, about 80 percent of all fire fatalities—more than 4,000—occur in homes and apartments. This is 1 death every 2 hours in the United States. Every 97 minutes, a fire kills somebody in the United States. SOURCE: NATIONAL FIRE PROTECTION ASSOCIATION.

Dangerous Fun

Fireworks were responsible for 6,270 injuries in 1989. Firecrackers caused 39 percent of the injuries, sparklers 19 percent, bottle rockets 12 percent, shells 6 percent, fountains 5 percent, ground spinners 3 percent, and missiles 1 percent. Homemade, public display, and others caused 15 percent of the injuries.
SOURCE: CONSUMER PRODUCT SAFETY COMMISSION.

Frequency of Accidents

The incidence of home accidents is 1 every 9 seconds. On-the-job accidents occur 1 every 18 seconds. Motor vehicle accidents occur at the rate of 1 every 18 seconds.

SOURCE: *ACCIDENT FACTS*, 1989 EDITION.

Expensive Accidents

A serious accident usually means a trip to the hospital, where the average cost per patient is more than $580 per day.

SOURCE: *HOSPITAL STATISTICS*, 1989 EDITION, PUBLISHED BY THE AMERICAN HOSPITAL ASSOCIATION.

High-School Athletic Injuries

Of the 5.8 million high-school athletes, an estimated 1 million are injured each year, nearly 1 out of 6!

SOURCE: CORDNER NELSON. *CAREERS IN PRO SPORTS.* ROSEN PUBLISHING GROUP, 1990.

Accidental Deaths

Every 10 minutes, 2 people die in car crashes and 170 are injured.

SOURCE: NATIONAL SAFETY COUNCIL ESTIMATES.

Abundance of Injuries

Each day more than 170,000 men, women, and children are seriously injured; nearly 400 die as a result of their injuries.

SOURCE: NATIONAL SAFETY COUNCIL. *INJURY PREVENTION: MEETING THE CHALLENGE*. NATIONAL CENTER FOR HEALTH STATISTICS, U.S. GOVERNMENT PRINTING OFFICE, 1987.

Disabled by Accidents

Each year 50,000 children are disabled as a result of an accident.

SOURCE: ALAN DOELP. *IN THE BLINK OF AN EYE*. PRENTICE HALL PRESS, 1989.

Drunk Driving and Youth

More than 40 percent of all 15- to 19-year-old fatalities result from motor vehicle crashes. About half of these were in alcohol-related crashes. Estimates are that 3,158 persons in this age group died in alcohol-related crashes in 1988.

In 1988, nearly 27 percent of all fatally injured 15- to 19-year-old drivers were intoxicated.

SOURCE: U.S. DEPARTMENT OF TRANSPORTATION, NATIONAL HIGHWAY TRAFFIC SAFETY ADMINISTRATION.

Suffering Cyclists

On average, a cyclist involved in a motor vehicle collision will suffer:

1.4 days in the hospital
1.4 days in bed at home
4.3 days missed from school
23.6 days of pain and discomfort

SOURCE: IBID.

Fatal Crashes

With about 42,119 fatal crashes in the nation in 1988, 24,711 crashes involved only 1 vehicle, and 17,408 involved 2 or more vehicles.

With a total of about 62,686 vehicles involved in fatal crashes in 1988, 36,944 were passenger cars and 13,585 were light trucks.

With a total of 47,093 persons killed in fatal crashes in 1988, 27,260 were drivers, 11,805 passengers, 113 others, and 7,915 nonoccupants.

Males outnumber females as fatal crash victims by an average of 2 to 1.

Almost half of all fatalities occur on weekends.

SOURCE: NATIONAL HIGHWAY TRAFFIC SAFETY ADMINISTRATION'S FATAL ACCIDENT REPORTING SYSTEM.

Abundance of Head Injuries

More than 2 million head injuries occur each year, with more than a half million severe enough to require hospital admission. Every 15 seconds someone receives a head injury, every 5 minutes one of these people will die and another will become permanently disabled.

SOURCE: NATIONAL HEAD INJURY FOUNDATION.

Cost of Brain Injury

A survivor of a severe brain injury typically faces 5 to 10 years of intensive care at an estimated cost of more than $4 million.

SOURCE: IBID.

Getting Fried

Lightning strikes the earth 100 times each second. In 1989, 70 people died from lightning. 29 percent of all lightning deaths occur during the month of July. SOURCE: NATIONAL WEATHER SERVICE.

Final Exits in United States

In 1991, there were 2,033,000 deaths by natural causes, 94,000 accidental deaths, and 28,000 suicides.

SOURCE: AL NEUHARTH, "PLAIN TALK," *USA TODAY*, AUGUST 16, 1991.

Don't Say No to These Drugs

Due to heart disease alone, it is estimated that 125,000 people a year die because they don't take their medicine as prescribed. SOURCE: NATIONAL PHARMACEUTICAL COUNCIL.

Booze Is Good for the Heart

Although the consumption of alcohol may be bad for your liver, a 1991 report based on a study of 51,000 men states that men who consume from ½ to 2 drinks a day reduce their risk of heart disease by 26 percent as compared with men who abstain from alcohol. SOURCE: *LANCET* (A U.K. MEDICAL JOURNAL).

Most Common Causes of Household Fires

- Roofs of rural or outlying homes are especially vulnerable to the nearly 500,000 wildfires a year.
- Attics and concealed spaces are the origin of more than 26,000 fires and cause 95 deaths a year. Electrical systems are to blame for 45,000 home fires and 430 deaths.

- More deaths from home fires occur between 2 and 3 A.M. than any other time.
- Cigarettes and other smoking paraphernalia are the leading cause of home-fire fatalities—killing 1,300 people a year.
- The kitchen is the number one room in the house where fires originate. Cooking equipment causes the highest incidence of home-fire injuries—an average of 4,380 a year.
- Heating equipment is the most frequent cause of home fires and more than 740 deaths a year.
- Improper use of candles leads to more than 1,800 fires and 40 deaths a year.
- Balconies and porches account for 7,500 fires and 41 deaths a year. SOURCE: NATIONAL FIRE PROTECTION ASSOCIATION.

Cancer Strikes

Cancer is responsible for about 1 death per minute in the United States. More than 1 million new cases were diagnosed in 1991. Protection from sun's rays could have prevented 540,000 skin cancers. SOURCE: AMERICAN CANCER SOCIETY.

I'll Quit Smoking

Only 5% of all high-school seniors who smoke think they will still smoke later in their lives, when, in fact, after 8 years, 75% still do. SOURCE: IBID.

Tobacco Kills

Somewhere in the world, every 15 seconds, a person dies from a tobacco-related illness. SOURCE: IBID.

$23,000 a Second on Medical Care

Americans spend $23,000 every second on medical care, more than $2 billion a day.

SOURCE: JANICE CASTRO, "CONDITION: CRITICAL," *TIME*, NOVEMBER 25, 1991, P. 34.

7. Time and Crime

A Night in the Slammer

3 percent of females and 20 percent of males have spent a night in jail. SOURCE: TOM AND NANCY BIRACREE. *ALMANAC OF THE AMERICAN PEOPLE*. FACTS ON FILE, 1988.

Male Kidnappers Serve Longer

Female prisoners convicted of kidnapping are released from state prison after serving an average of 32 months. Males serve an average of 39 months. SOURCE: *SOURCEBOOK OF CRIMINAL JUSTICE STATISTICS—1987*. U.S. DEPARTMENT OF JUSTICE.

Time for Motor Vehicle Theft

Female prisoners convicted of motor vehicle theft are released from prison after serving an average of 15 months. Males serve an average of 16 months. SOURCE: IBID.

Black Males Doing Time

Nearly 1 out of 4 black males in his twenties is behind bars, on probation, or parole. SOURCE: THE SENTENCING PROJECT.

S & L Scams

The average savings and loan offender in 1989 was sentenced to 1.9 years, whereas the average bank robber was sentenced to 9.4 years.

SOURCE: FBI.

Youngsters Going Back for More

More than 75 percent of those 17 and younger when released from prison are rearrested. 52 percent of females and 70 percent of males paroled from prison between the ages of 17 and 22 are rearrested within 6 years.

SOURCE: U.S. DEPARTMENT OF JUSTICE.

Average Age of Arrest (1985)

CHARGE	AVERAGE AGE
Gambling	37 years
Murder	30 years
Sex offense	30 years
Fraud	30 years
Embezzlement	29 years
Aggravated assault	29 years
Forcible rape	28 years
Weapons	28 years
Forgery	27 years
Drug abuse violations	26 years
Stolen property	25 years
Theft	25 years
Arson	24 years
Robbery	24 years
Burglary	22 years
Motor vehicle theft	22 years

SOURCE: AGE-SPECIFIC ARREST RATES AND RACE-SPECIFIC ARREST RATES FOR SELECTED OFFENSES, 1965–1985, FBI UNIFORM CRIME REPORTING PROGRAM, DECEMBER 1986.

Oldest Prisoner

Bill Wallace shot and killed a man at a restaurant in Melbourne, Victoria, Australia, in December 1925. He spent 63 years at the Aradale Psychiatric Hospital at Ararat, Victoria, until he died on July 17, 1989, shortly before his 108th birthday.

SOURCE: *GUINNESS BOOK OF WORLD RECORDS*, 1990.

Time Confined

State prisons housing females confine inmates to their units 9.9 hours a day. Prisons housing males confine inmates 11.4 hours a day.

SOURCE: *SOURCEBOOK OF CRIMINAL JUSTICE STATISTICS—1987*. U.S. DEPARTMENT OF JUSTICE.

Longest Jail Term Served

Paul Geidel was convicted of second-degree murder on September 5, 1911, as a 17-year-old porter in a New York hotel. He served 68 years, 8 months, and 2 days at the Fishkill Correctional Facility, Beacon, New York. He was released on May 7, 1980 at age 85. He first refused parole in 1974.

SOURCE: *GUINNESS BOOK OF WORLD RECORDS*, 1990.

Time in the Slammer

The average time spent incarcerated is 4 years, 10 months; the median sentence is about 3 years. State prisons have an average stay of 6 years, 9 months; whereas local jails have an average stay of 9 months.

SOURCE: NATIONAL JUDICIAL REPORTING PROGRAM OF BUREAU OF JUSTICE STATISTICS.

Time for Convicted Felons

TYPE OF CRIME	AVERAGE TIME SENTENCED
Murder and nonnegligent manslaughter	7 years, 2 months
Rape	5 years, 6 months
Robbery	4 years, 9 months
Burglary	2 years, 7 months
Drug trafficking	1 year, 10 months

SOURCE: IBID.

The Prison Population

In 1989 there were 679,263 criminals in institutions sentenced to more than 1 year. That's 47,168 in federal institutions and 632,095 in state institutions. 5 people in federal institutions were under sentence of death, and 2,205 from state institutions were under the death sentence.

SOURCE: PRISON POPULATION: BUREAU OF JUSTICE STATISTICS, U.S. DEPARTMENT OF JUSTICE, DECEMBER 31, 1989. DEATH PENALTY: NAACP LEGAL DEFENSE AND EDUCATION FUND. "UNDER SENTENCE OF DEATH" AS OF JULY 1989.

Serving More Than a Year

The chance of being sentenced for more than a year in prison for those arrested for:

Homicide, 49 percent
Rape, 29 percent
Robbery, 28 percent
Burglary, 20 percent
Motor vehicle theft, 7 percent

SOURCE: U.S. DEPARTMENT OF JUSTICE, BUREAU OF JUSTICE STATISTICS.

Longest Death Row

Sadamichi Hirasawa remained on death row for 39 years in Sendai Jail, Japan. He was convicted in 1948 of poisoning 12 bank employees with potassium cyanide to effect a theft; he died at the age of 94.

SOURCE: *GUINNESS BOOK OF WORLD RECORDS*, 1990.

Longest Sentence for Mass Murder

Juan Corona received a sentence of 25 consecutive life terms in jail for killing 25 farm workers in 1970 and 1971.

SOURCE: IBID.

Deliver Those Letters!

A sentence of 384,912 years was demanded at the prosecution of Gabriel March Grandos for failing to deliver 42,768 letters—a sentence of 9 years per letter. He was prosecuted at Palma de Mallorca, Spain, on March 11, 1972.

SOURCE: IBID.

How Much Longer?

36 percent of Americans on death row have been there for more than 4 years.

SOURCE: *STATISTICAL ABSTRACT OF THE UNITED STATES—1987*. BUREAU OF THE CENSUS. U.S. DEPARTMENT OF COMMERCE.

Waiting to Die

The average time spent on death row is 6 years and 8 months for those who are executed. The median time for all prisoners on death row is 3 years and 9 months.

SOURCE: U.S. DEPARTMENT OF JUSTICE.

Day Burglaries

About 37 percent of no-force burglaries are known to have occurred between 6 A.M. and 6 P.M.

SOURCE: REPORT TO THE NATION ON CRIME AND JUSTICE, BUREAU OF JUSTICE STATISTICS.

Night-Time Crime

54 percent of all robberies in the United States are committed during the night.

SOURCE: UNIFORM CRIME REPORTS: CRIME IN THE UNITED STATES—1986. FEDERAL BUREAU OF INVESTIGATION. U.S. DEPARTMENT OF JUSTICE.

Lock Your Doors—Especially in August and December

Robberies are most likely to occur in August and December and least likely to occur in February and April.

SOURCE: REPORT TO THE NATION ON CRIME AND JUSTICE.

Household Burglaries

The odds of a household being burglarized over a 20-year period is 72 percent, larceny 89 percent, and a motor vehicle theft 19 percent.

SOURCE: *LIFETIME LIKELIHOOD OF VICTIMIZATION.* BUREAU OF JUSTICE STATISTICS TECHNICAL REPORT, MARCH 1987.

It's a Crime

In 1989, about 1 out of 4 households suffered a violent crime or property crime. This includes attempted and completed crimes.

SOURCE: BUREAU OF JUSTICE STATISTICS.

Don't Walk Alone at Night

73 percent of rapes occur between 6 P.M. and 6 A.M.

SOURCE: REPORT TO THE NATION ON CRIME AND JUSTICE.

Seizing Cocaine

The Drug Enforcement Agency seized 56,980 kilograms of cocaine in 1988, 50 percent more than in 1987.

SOURCE: *STATISTICAL ABSTRACT OF THE UNITED STATES.*

Victims of Violent Crimes

An estimated five-sixths of Americans will be victims of attempted or completed violent crimes during our lives. The risk is greater for males than females and for blacks than whites.

SOURCE: *LIFETIME LIKELIHOOD OF VICTIMIZATION,* BUREAU OF JUSTICE STATISTICS TECHNICAL REPORT, MARCH 1987.

Lifetime Risk of Homicide

Lifetime risk of being a victim of homicide: 1 out of 179 for white males, 1 out of 30 for black males, 1 out of 495 for white females, and 1 out of 132 for black females.

SOURCE: UPDATED DATA BASED ON SIMILAR MATERIAL FROM *THE RISK OF VIOLENT CRIME*, BUREAU OF JUSTICE STATISTICS SPECIAL REPORT, MAY 1985.

The Thieving Thirties

12 percent of all Americans age 30 to 34 are arrested during a single year. SOURCE: *SOURCEBOOK OF CRIMINAL JUSTICE STATISTICS—1986*. U.S. DEPARTMENT OF JUSTICE.

High-School Shoplifters

An estimated 27 percent of American high-school seniors shoplifted in a given year. SOURCE: UNIFORM CRIME REPORTS: CRIME IN THE UNITED STATES—1986. FEDERAL BUREAU OF INVESTIGATION. U.S. DEPARTMENT OF JUSTICE.

Longest Escape

Leonard T. Fristoe escaped from the Nevada State Prison on December 15, 1923, and was turned in by his son on November 15, 1969 at Compton, California. He had 46 years of freedom under the name of Claude R. Willis. He originally went to jail for killing two sheriff's deputies in 1920.

SOURCE: *GUINNESS BOOK OF WORLD RECORDS*, 1990.

Annual Murders

3,100 white females and 1,900 black females are murdered each year; 8,600 white males and 7,600 black males are murdered each year.

SOURCE: *STATISTICAL ABSTRACT OF THE UNITED STATES—1989*. BUREAU OF THE CENSUS.

Annual Arrests

1,914,000 females and 8,882,000 males are arrested each year.

SOURCE: IBID.

Arrested for Rape

350 females and 28,000 males are arrested for rape each year.

SOURCE: *UNIFORM CRIME REPORTS: CRIME IN THE UNITED STATES—1988*. FEDERAL BUREAU OF INVESTIGATION, U.S. DEPARTMENT OF JUSTICE.

Lifetime Chances of Being Raped

Nearly 1 out of 12 females will be the victim of a completed or attempted rape sometime during their lives.

SOURCE: U.S. DEPARTMENT OF JUSTICE.

A Burglar's Salary

The average burglar earns $50 an hour, assuming the average heist takes 2 hours and nets roughly $100 after the goods are fenced. But those wages drop to 33 cents an hour when they are divided by the average prison sentence that convicted burglars receive. SOURCE: BRIAN DUMAINE, "NEW WEAPONS," *FORTUNE*, JUNE 3, 1991.

Gun Manufacturing

In 1989, U.S. gun manufacturers pumped out more than 4 million nonmilitary firearms. That's 1,376,000 pistols, 622,000 revolvers, 1,382,000 rifles, and 688,000 shotguns.

SOURCE: ALAN FARNHAM, "INSIDE THE U.S. GUN BUSINESS," *FORTUNE*, JUNE 3, 1991.

Even Small Dealers Make Money

Small-time street drug dealers in Washington, D.C., gross an average of $48,000 a year. They net $24,000 tax-free after paying for the drugs and their runners.

SOURCE: PETER VEUTER AND ROBERT MACCOUN OF RAND CORP.

Expensive Law Enforcement

The United States spends some $50 billion a year (that's $240 per man, woman, and child) on all aspects of law enforcement. If the United States keeps throwing people in prison in the 1990s at the rate of the 1980s, some 250 new cells a day will be needed. That's at least $5 billion a year for construction costs alone.

SOURCE: NORVAL MORRIS, A UNIVERSITY OF CHICAGO LAW SCHOOL PROFESSOR.

World Murder Rates

During the late 1980s, the U.S. murder rate was 8.9 per 100,000 people per year.

Venezuela's murder rate was 8.9; Canada's was 7.7; West Germany's was 9; England's, Wales', and Japan's were 0.6 per 100,000 people per year.

SOURCE: *1990 WORLD HEALTH STATISTICS ANNUAL.*

Violent Crimes

The U.S. population has grown 41 percent since 1960, whereas violent crimes have increased 516 percent. Fewer than 35 Americans became the victims of violent criminals every hour in 1960. Currently about 200 Americans are victimized every hour.

SOURCE: FBI AND U.S. CENSUS STATISTICS.

Rates of Victimization Over a 20-Year Period

Percent of households that will be victimized in a 20-year period:

	BURGLARY	LARCENY	MOTOR VEHICLE THEFT
All households	72%	89%	19%
Urban	80%	93%	27%
Suburban	70%	90%	20%
Rural	64%	82%	11%

SOURCE: *LIFETIME LIKELIHOOD OF VICTIMIZATION*, BUREAU OF JUSTICE STATISTICS TECHNICAL REPORT, MARCH 1987.

Elderly Abuse

An estimated 1.1 million elderly Americans are abused annually and of these nearly 85 percent are abused by members of their own family. SOURCE: THE UNITED WAY OF AMERICA.

Battered Spouses

Each year between 2 million and 6 million women are battered, and of these, 3 in 4 victims of spouse abuse were divorced or separated at the time of the abuse.

SOURCE: NATIONAL COALITION AGAINST DOMESTIC VIOLENCE.

Killings in the United States

The nation's citizens committed a record number of murders in 1990—at least 23,000 or nearly 3 an hour! The U.S. murder rate is more than double that of Northern Ireland, which is torn by civil war; it's 4 times that of Italy, 9 times that of England, and 11 times that of Japan. SOURCE: SENATE JUDICIARY COMMITTEE REPORT.

The U.S. Murder Capitals

Homicides per 100,000 people per year:

CITY	RATE*
Washington, DC	70.4
Detroit	51.0

CITY	RATE*
New Orleans	51.0
Dallas	37.2
Baltimore	34.8
Boston	31.8
Jacksonville, FL	30.2
New York	29.4
Houston	29.0
Chicago	27.2

*Figures for first 6 months of 1990 at an annual rate.

SOURCE: NEW YORK CITY POLICE DEPARTMENT.

Problems at School (How Times Have Changed)

Leading school discipline problems:

1940	1989
Talking	Drug Abuse
Chewing gum	Alcohol abuse
Making noise	Pregnancy
Running in the hallways	Suicide
Getting out of place in line	Rape
Wearing improper clothing	Assault
Not putting paper in wastebaskets	Burglary
	Bombings

SOURCE: THIS COMPARISON IS THE RESULT OF A STUDY CONDUCTED BY THE FULLERTON, CALIFORNIA, POLICE DEPARTMENT AND THE CALIFORNIA DEPARTMENT OF EDUCATION.

Plead Guilty!

Here is the average sentence given after a:

	TRIAL BY JURY	TRIAL BY JUDGE	GUILTY PLEA
Murder	28 years	21 years	14 years
Robbery	24 years	15 years	10 years
Rape	18 years	14 years	11 years
Aggravated assault	14 years	9 years	7 years
Burglary	10 years	5 years	6 years

	TRIAL BY JURY	TRIAL BY JUDGE	GUILTY PLEA
Drug trafficking	8 years	10 years	5 years
Larceny	4 years	4 years	4 years

SOURCE: U.S. DEPARTMENT OF JUSTICE.

Waiting on Death Row

At year end, 1990, 2,356 prisoners awaited execution on death row in the United States. There were 32 women, and the median age was 34. Of those condemned to die, 1,375 (58.4 percent) were white, 943 (40 percent) were black, 24 (1 percent) were Native American, and 14 (0.6 percent) were Asian. Those of Hispanic ethnic origin totaled 172 (7.3 percent).

SOURCE: BUREAU OF JUSTICE STATISTICS.

Death Row Executions

Since 1976, 3,834 people have been sentenced to die, but only 143 (3.7 percent) had been executed by the end of 1990.

SOURCE: IBID.

Average Length of Jury Deliberations

The average length of time that juries spend deliberating in order to reach a verdict in criminal trials is as follows:

CRIME	HOURS & MINUTES
Homicide	5 hr., 30 min.
Rape	3 hr., 40 min.
Aggravated assault	2 hr., 38 min.
Burglary	2 hr., 19 min.
Narcotics	2 hr., 12 min.
Robbery	1 hr. 50 min.
Theft	1 hr. 40 min.

SOURCE: NATIONAL CENTER FOR STATE COURTS (BASED ON COMPARATIVE STUDY OF 9 COURTS IN NEW JERSEY, COLORADO, AND CALIFORNIA).

8. Time and Nature

5 Billion and Counting

As of mid-1990, there were about 5.3 billion members of the human family on the earth. Every year, another 145 million or so more people are born. This averages about 12 million per month, 2.7 million a week, 395,000 a day, 16,000 an hour, 275 a minute, and 4.6 a second!

About 51 million people die each year, or about 1.6 a second, leaving a natural increase of about 93 million people a year, or about 3 per second.

SOURCE: POPULATION REFERENCE BUREAU'S 1990 WORLD POPULATION DATA SHEET.

Population Doubling Rate

Africa's population of 601 million has a doubling time of 24 years.

Asia's population of 2.9 billion has a doubling time of 37 years.

North America's population of 270 million has a doubling time of 101 years.

Latin America's population of 421 million has a doubling time of 31 years.

Europe has a population of 495 million and a doubling time of 272 years.

The Commonwealth of Independent States (the former Soviet Union) has a population of 284 million and a doubling time of 79 years.

Australia, New Zealand, and the South Pacific islands have a population of 25 million and a doubling time of 59 years.

SOURCE: POPULATION REFERENCE BUREAU, INC., 1987.

A Million More People

Every 4 days the world's population increases by 1 million people

SOURCE: AUTHORS' CALCULATIONS.

Deadly Storms

Deaths from storms totaled 276 during the 1-year period from September 1987 through August 1988. Lightning killed 72, floods killed 35, tornadoes 33, thunderstorm winds 22, and high winds 17. The greatest number of deaths by storms occurred in August.

SOURCE: NATIONAL CLIMATIC DATA CENTER.

Dangerous Storms

From September 1987 through August 1988, 1,909 people were injured as a result of storms. Tornadoes injured 847, lightning 343, and thunderstorm winds 328. July had the greatest number of injuries from lightning and November had the greatest number from tornadoes.

SOURCE: IBID.

Our Crowded Planet in 2060

Those newborns who arrived in 1990 will live on a crowded planet when they reach age 70. The world's population in 1990 was 5.3 billion and will increase to 10.8 billion by 2060.

SOURCE: POPULATION REFERENCE BUREAU.

The Speed of Light

Light travels at the rate of 186,000 miles per second. The moon is about 250,000 miles from the earth, a little more than a "light second" away. If you turned on a flashlight on one side of the Milky Way, the light wouldn't reach the other end for 1,000 years. SOURCE: TOM BURNS, COLUMBUS ASTRONOMICAL SOCIETY.

Beware of Poisonous Ladies Who Bite

In 1989, 2,350 cases of black widow spider bites were reported in the United States. Tucson is the nation's black widow capital, where 1 in 5 of these cases was reported. Arizona accounted for about 1,000 of the reported bites.

SOURCE: AMERICAN ASSOCIATION OF POISON CONTROL CENTERS.

Hitting Puberty

Adolescent girls reach puberty at about 12 years of age compared with age 14 for boys.

SOURCE: *MASTERS AND JOHNSON ON SEX AND HUMAN LOVING.* LITTLE, BROWN, 1986.

Destruction of Rain Forests

The destruction of tropical rain forests is killing off at least 4,000 wild species a year. Rain forests are now about 55 percent of their original size, and the rate of loss in 1989 was almost double that of 1979. At current rates, one-quarter or more of the species of organisms on earth could be eliminated within 50 years.

SOURCE: ANITA MANNING, "THE DIRE RESULTS OF RAIN FOREST DESTRUCTION," *USA TODAY*, AUGUST 16, 1991.

Save Our Rain Forests

Each year, 27 million acres of tropical rain forests are destroyed. That's an area the size of Ohio, and translates to 74,000 acres per day, 3,000 acres per hour, and 50 acres per minute.

SOURCE: THE RAINFOREST ACTION NETWORK.

Soil Erosion

More than 3 million acres of productive farmland are lost to development each year or about 320 acres of agricultural land per hour. SOURCE: THE AMERICAN FARMLAND TRUST.

Large Hearts, More Beats

A human's heart weight is .42 percent of body weight, and the pulse rate at rest averages 72 beats per minute. A house sparrow's heart is 1.68 percent of body weight and the pulse rate at rest is 460 beats per minute. The tiny ruby-throated hummingbird has a pulse rate of 615 beats per minute.

SOURCE: *THE BIRDS AROUND US*. ORTHO BOOKS, SAN FRANCISCO, CA, 1986.

Speedy Birds

Most small birds fly at air speeds of about 20 mph except the hummingbird, which flaps its wings more than 70 times a second and can reach speeds of 60 mph in a tail wind. Waterfowl and the large seabirds maintain speeds of 40 mph or more. Migrating birds propel themselves at moderate speeds, relying on the weather and winds for flight. SOURCE: IBID.

Dodo Birds?

These fat, lumpy flightless birds were bigger than turkeys and laid only 1 large white egg per year. The dodo's home was the volcanic island of Mauritius in the Indian Ocean until the Portuguese discovered it and drove this helpless bird to its extinction in the late seventeenth century.

SOURCE: *ACADEMIC AMERICAN ENCYCLOPEDIA*.

Fastest Marine Animal

In 1958 a killer whale was timed at 34.5 mph in the eastern Pacific. SOURCE: *GUINNESS BOOK OF WORLD RECORDS*, 1990.

Fastest Land Animal

The fastest of all land animals is the cheetah, which can run at about 60 to 65 mph over a short distance on level ground. The fastest land animal over a sustained distance (i.e., over 1,000 yards) is the pronghorn antelope, which has been clocked at 35 mph for 4 miles, at 42 mph for 1 mile, and up to 55 mph for half a mile.

SOURCE: IBID.

Slowest Moving Mammal

The slowest moving land animal is the three-toed sloth, which averages 6 to 8 feet per minute. The slowest swimming marine animal is the sea otter, which reaches a top speed of 6 mph.

SOURCE: IBID.

Longest Hibernation

The barrow ground squirrel hibernates for 9 months a year in Point Barrow, Alaska.

SOURCE: IBID.

Longest and Shortest Gestation Periods

The longest gestation period for mammals is the Asiatic elephant with an average of 609 days and a maximum of 760 days. The shortest gestation period for mammals is the rare water opposum and the American opposum, both with gestation periods averaging 12 to 13 days, but as few as 8 days.

SOURCE: IBID.

The Big Bang

The big bang occurred 13 to 15 billion years ago.

SOURCE: *SCIENTIFIC AMERICAN*, OCTOBER 1990:
THE ALMANAC OF SCIENCE AND TECHNOLOGY.

Eclipses

Eclipses occur nearly every year somewhere on the earth, but a total solar eclipse is not always easy to observe from any given spot on earth. For example, London hasn't seen an eclipse since 1715 and won't see another until the twenty-sixth century. San Diego experienced one in 1923 and New York in 1925, but the next one won't occur in the United States until August 21, 2017.

SOURCE: BOB BENMAN, "THE GREAT BAJA ECLIPSE," *DISCOVER*, JANUARY 1991.

Oldest Tree

The oldest tree was a bristlecone pine that grew on the northeast face of Mt. Wheeler in eastern Nevada. It was cut down by a chain saw when it was about 5,100 years old.

SOURCE: *GUINNESS BOOK OF WORLD RECORDS*, 1990.

Fastest-Growing Trees

The Albizzia falcata grew 35 feet, 3 inches in 13 months in Sabah, Malaysia, in 1974. SOURCE: IBID.

Speed of Lightning

The speed of a discharge varies from 100 to 1,000 miles/second for the downward leader track, and reached up to 87,000 miles/second (nearly half the speed of light) for the powerful return stroke. SOURCE: IBID.

Going Extinct

Our planet is now losing up to 3 species per day. That figure is predicted to reach 3 species per hour in scarcely a decade. By the year 2000, 20 percent of the earth's species could be lost forever. SOURCE: THE NATURE CONSERVANCY.

Junk Mail

Americans receive almost 2 million tons of junk mail every year, adding up to about 100 million trees.

SOURCE: *50 SIMPLE THINGS YOU CAN DO TO SAVE THE EARTH*; THE EARTH WORKS GROUP.

Deadly Sunday Papers

It takes an entire forest—about 500,000 trees—to supply Americans with their Sunday newspapers every week

SOURCE: PAPER RECYCLING COMMITTEE.

Most Sunshine

The annual average of daily sunshine in Yuma, Arizona, is 90 percent (more than 4,000 hours). St. Petersburg, Florida, recorded 768 consecutive sunny days from February 9, 1967, to March 17, 1969. SOURCE: *GUINNESS BOOK OF WORLD RECORDS*, 1991.

Greatest Rainfall

A record of 73.62 inches of rain fell in 24 hours in Cilaos, La Réunion, an island in the Indian Ocean, on March 15 and 16, 1952. The record for a calendar month is 366.14 inches at Cherrapunji, Meghalaya, India, in July 1861. In the United States, the 24-hour record is 19 inches at Alvin, Texas, on July 25–26, 1979. During a 12-month period, 739 inches fell at Kukui, Maui, from December 1981 to December 1982. SOURCE: IBID.

Tornadoes

A tornado has a maximum life span of up to 9 hours but can travel up to 300 miles during this time.

SOURCE: FRANK KENDIG AND RICHARD HUTTON. *LIFE-SPANS OR HOW LONG THINGS LAST*. HOLT, RINEHART AND WINSTON, 1979.

Lightning

Lightning lasts between 45 and 55 microseconds.

SOURCE: IBID.

Cut Flowers

If premium conditions are provided, fresh-cut roses can last an average of 7 to 10 days, carnations about 2 weeks, gladiolus 7 to 10 days, and pompons 2 weeks. Flowers purchased from a florist last an average of 2 to 3 days less. SOURCE: IBID.

The Universe

According to astronomers' estimates, the universe is now about 20 billion years old. SOURCE: IBID.

Galaxies

The galaxies, including our own Milky Way, were formed 10 to 100 million years after the explosion that marked the beginning of our universe. SOURCE: IBID.

The Sun

The sun is estimated to be about 4 to 5 billion years old. This medium-sized star has a life span of about 10 billion years.

SOURCE: IBID.

Sunbeams

It takes about 8.3 minutes for a beam of light to travel from the sun to the earth. SOURCE: IBID.

Moonbeams

It only takes about 1.3 seconds for moonlight to reach the earth. SOURCE: IBID.

Early Menstruation

The average age at which girls begin to menstruate is 12.9, down from 14.3 in 1900. SOURCE: DR. J. M. TANNER. *GROWTH OF ADOLESCENCE*. CHARLES THOMAS, 1962.

Human Life Expectancy

At birth a female is expected to live 78.3 years. A male is expected to live 71.3 years.

SOURCE: *STATISTICAL ABSTRACT OF THE UNITED STATES 1989*. BUREAU OF THE CENSUS.

In 1900, the life expectancy for a female was 48.3 years and 46.3 years for a male. For a nonwhite female it was 33.5 and for a nonwhite male it was 32.5. SOURCE: *HISTORICAL STATISTICS OF THE UNITED STATES—COLONIAL TIMES TO 1970*. BUREAU OF THE CENSUS.

Sperm Survival in a Woman's Body

Sperm can survive for about 8 days in a woman's body.

SOURCE: KINSEY INSTITUTE FOR RESEARCH IN SEX, GENDER AND REPRODUCTION.

Sperm Finds an Egg Quickly

It takes about 5 minutes for sperm, once inside a woman's body, to reach an egg. SOURCE: IBID.

An Enormous Daily Diet

A fully grown elephant eats during most of its waking hours, and consumes up to 660 pounds of grass, leaves, and twigs daily. SOURCE: ASSOCIATED PRESS.

How Long Is a Year?

The earth is following its elliptical orbit around the sun at 19 miles per second, or 68,000 mph. Astronomers define various types of years, but the most familiar one is the tropical year, which is based on seasons. Lasting 365 days, 5 hours, 48 minutes, and 46 seconds, the tropical year brought about leap year in order to bring the solar calendar into step with the lunar calendar.

SOURCE: DAVID WALLECHINSKY AND IRVING WALLACE. *THE PEOPLE'S ALMANAC #3*. BANTAM BOOKS, 1981.

Preservation of Body Parts

Blood: The American Red Cross refrigerates blood for 3 weeks; after that time the blood is turned over to laboratories for research.

Corneas: Maximum storage life is 3 to 4 days in a tissue culture and 6 months to a year when frozen.

Kidneys: Kidneys can last up to 18 hours in a cold electrolyte solution or up to 72 hours in the pulsatile perfusion technique, which pumps cold oxygen through the kidneys.

Liver: A human liver can be maintained in a transplantable condition for 2 to 8 hours.

Heart: A live human heart can be kept in perfect condition for as long as 4 hours after removal if an electrolyte solution is pumped through its blood vessels.

Bone marrow: Stored at -50°C, marrow can be kept fresh for 6 months to a year.

Sperm: Healthy, normal babies have been carried by mothers artificially impregnated with sperm that had been kept frozen for as long as 13 years.

SOURCE: FRANK KENDIG AND RICHARD HUTTON. *LIFE-SPANS OR HOW LONG THINGS LAST*. HOLT, RINEHART AND WINSTON, 1979.

Oldest Caged Pets

Hamster: A golden hamster lived for 19 years in Cambridge, England.

Rabbit: Flopsy lived for more than 19 years, 10 months in Tasmania.

Guinea pig: Snowball lived for 14 years, 10½ months in Nottinghamshire, England.

Gerbil: A Mongolian gerbil named Sahara lived for 8 years, 4½ months in Michigan.

Mouse: A house mouse lived for 7 years, 7 months in England.

Rat: A rat lived for 5 years, 8 months in Philadelphia.

SOURCE: *GUINNESS BOOK OF WORLD RECORDS*, 1990.

Fastest Reptile

The fastest-moving land reptile is 18 mph by a 6-lined race runner. The highest speed attained by any reptile in water is 22 mph by a Pacific leatherback turtle. SOURCE: IBID.

A Long Journey for Warmth

Each year, willow warblers weighing only a few grams travel about 5,000 miles to escape the hardships of winter.

SOURCE: ROBIN BAKER, ED. *THE MYSTERY OF MIGRATION*. VIKING PRESS, 1981.

A Long Flight

Many strong-flying insects, such as butterflies, moths, and locusts migrate across the country throughout their adult lives, traveling as far as 600 miles from their places of birth. Birds, on the other hand, migrate much farther. The Arctic tern performs a transglobal migration twice a year, covering more than 25,000 miles. To complete this journey from one pole to another it must fly nonstop for 8 months of the year and plunge into the water for fish en route. SOURCE: IBID.

Oldest Animals

Bat: The oldest-known bat is 32 years old. This little brown bat was banded in the United States in 1987.

Orangutan: Excluding man, Guas is the oldest known primate, living to be 59 years old.

Monkey: The oldest monkey was a male white-throated capuchin called Bobo who lived to be 53 years of age.

Rodent: A Sumatran crested porcupine lived to be 27 years, 3 months in the National Zoological Park, Washington, D.C.

Antelope: The oldest reliable recorded age was 25 years, 4 months for an addax, which died in the Brookfield Zoo, Chicago.

Deer: The oldest deer is a red deer that lived to be 26 years, 8 months.

Horse: The oldest horse was Old Billy, who lived to be 62 years of age.

Dog: An Australian cattle dog named Bluey lived for 29 years, 5 months.

Cat: Puss, the oldest cat ever recorded, lived to be 36 years of age.

Bird: The oldest reported bird was the sulphur-crested cockatoo, which lived to be 80+. The longest lived domestic bird (excluding the ostrich) is the domestic goose named George, which lived to be 49 years, 8 months.

Crocodile: The greatest age for a crocodile is 66 years for a female American alligator at the Adelaide Zoo, Australia.

Lizard: A male slowworm lived to be 54 years old in the Zoological Museum in Copenhagen, Denmark.

SOURCE: *GUINNESS BOOK OF WORLD RECORDS*, 1990.

Life Spans of Mammals

Aardvarks: These long-eared, long-nosed African anteaters live up to 10 years in captivity.

Antelopes: Eland have life expectancies of 15 to 20 years, and gazelles have life spans of 10 to 20 years.

Baboons: Baboons live for a maximum of 20 years in the wild, but there are some instances of baboons living more than 40 years in captivity.

Bats: The only flying mammals, bats can live 20 years or longer.

Bears: Black, brown, grizzly, and polar bears live 15 to 34 years in the wild.

Bobcats: Bobcats live up to 20 years in the wild.

Buffalo: The Asiatic buffalo lives up to 10 to 20 years and the American bison lives 18 to 22 years.

Camels: Camels can live up to 45 years.

Cats: The longest lived of the small domestic animals, cats have life spans of 13 to 17 years.

Cattle: Domestic cattle have potential life spans of more than 20 years, but cattle and steers raised for beef are usually slaughtered around their second birthday and dairy cattle at about 8 or 9 years.

Chimpanzees: Chimps have life spans of 35 to 40 years.

Chipmunks: Chipmunks live about 5 years in the wild.

Coyotes: Coyotes manage to survive in the wild for about 10 years.

Deer: The 41 species of deer have life spans ranging from 10 to 20 years.

Elephants: The life span of the Asiatic and African elephant is 60 to 65 years.

Foxes: In captivity foxes can live from 12 to 14 years.

Gerbils: These popular pets live up to 5 years.

Giraffes: Giraffes have a life span of 15 to 20 years.

Goats: Goats live about 15 to 20 years.

Gophers: These rodents live from 2 to 5 years.

Gorillas: Gorillas are estimated to live 25 to 30 years in their natural habitats.

Guinea pigs: These rodents can live up to 7 years in captivity.

Hippopotamuses: The life span of a hippo is about 43 years.

Hogs: The domestic hog has a life span of about 20 years, and the wild hog can live to about 27 years.

Horses: In general, horses have life spans of 25 to 30 years.

Hyenas: Hyenas live about 25 years in the wild.

Jaguars: Jaguars can live up to 22 years.

Mice: The average life span of a mouse is less than 5 years.

Minks: Minks live up to 10 years in captivity.

Monkeys: The life span of monkeys differs by species.

Moose: Moose live about 20 years.

Mountain lions: In captivity, pumas can live as long as 19 years.

Opossums: Opossums live for about 2 years.

Orangutans: Orangutans have lived for 30 years in captivity but can probably live as long as 40 in the wild.

Pigs: Pigs live anywhere from 10 to 20 years.

Porcupines: These rodents live 10 to 15 years in the wild and about 20 years in captivity.

Porpoises: Depending on the species, porpoises live 25 to 50 years.

Prairie dogs: Prairie dogs live only 10 years.

Rabbits: Rabbits live only about 2 years in the wild and about 5 in captivity.

Racoons: Racoons live for about 10 years.

Rats: Rats live up to 6 years, but 1 female can produce 800 offspring.

Reindeer: Reindeer live about 15 years.

Rhinoceroses: These mammals live up to 50 years.

Seals: The fur seal lives about 7 years in the wild. Harbor seals can live more than 30 years and the gray seal can live more than 40 years.

Sheep: Domestic sheep have a life span of about 7 years. Wild sheep such as the bighorn live up to 20 years and ewes as long as 23 years.

Shrews: Shrews average only 12 to 18 months in the wild because they have so many enemies.

Skunks: Skunks live up to 10 years in captivity.

Squirrels: Squirrels can live up to 15 years in captivity.

Walruses: Walruses live up to 40 years in the wild.

Whales: The average life span of a whale is about 50 years.

Wildebeests: These African antelopes live about 16 years.

Wolves: Wolves live up to 16 years in captivity.

Zebras: Zebras live about 25 to 30 years in the wild, but have reached 40 in captivity.

SOURCE: FRANK KENDIG AND RICHARD HUTTON. *LIFE-SPANS OR HOW LONG THINGS LAST*. HOLT, RINEHART AND WINSTON, 1979.

Life Spans of Invertebrates

Ants: Ants have three castes—queens, which live up to 15 years; workers, which live up to 7 years; and males, which die soon after mating, which could be as little as 3 days.

Bees: A queen bee lives up to 6 years, a worker bee about 6 months, and males about 8 weeks.

Beetles: Beetles live from 1 to 3 years.

Clams: Clams found in U.S. waters live about 60 years, and the giant clam lives about 30 years.

Cockroaches: The Oriental cockroach, the black one most often seen, has a life span of about 40 days. The American cockroach lives about 200 days.

Crabs: Hermit crabs live about 11 to 12 years; blue crabs, 2 to 3 years; and Alaskan king crabs more than 15 years.

Crickets: The common field cricket has a life span of 9 to 14 weeks.

Earthworms: Earthworms live from 5 to 10 years.

Flies: The average life span for the common housefly is about 19 to 30 days.

Grasshoppers: The familiar green grasshopper lives about 5 months.

Lobsters: A 1.5-pound lobster, the popular eating size, is about 8 years old.

Mosquitoes: Mosquitoes that make it past the first day live no longer than 2 months.

Octopuses: The Mediterranean octopus has a maximum life span of about 10 years.

Oysters: Saltwater oysters live up to 10 years.

Snails: Land snails live up to 5 years.

Spiders: The maximum life span for most spiders is 4 to 7 years. Tarantulas have been known to live as long as 20 years.

SOURCE: IBID.

Life Spans of Birds

Blue jays: Blue jays live up to 14 years in the wild.

Canaries: Canaries can live up to 20 years.

Chickens: The domestic chicken has a life span of 8 to 14 years.

Doves: Doves live up to 30 years in captivity.

Geese: The longest lived domestic bird, geese survive about 25 years.

Hawks: Hawks generally live less than 15 years.

Mockingbirds: Mockingbirds survive more than 10 years in the wild.

Mynas: Myna birds can live up to 20 years.

Ostriches: Ostriches live about 25 years.

Parrots: Parrots live up to about 50 years.

Pelicans: Pelicans live more than 30 years in captivity.

Penguins: In captivity, penguins have an average life span of 34 years.

Sparrows: Sparrows live more than 20 years.

Storks: Storks live more than 35 years in captivity.

Swans: Swans live up to 70 years.

Swifts: Swifts, the fastest bird alive, live only about 12 years.

Woodpeckers: Woodpeckers live an average of 10 years.

SOURCE: IBID.

Life Spans of Fish

American eels: These fish have survived up to 60 years in captivity but usually live for 7 to 20 years.

Carp: A carp's life span ranges from 20 to 25 years, but they have lived up to 47 years in captivity.

Cod: Cod live about 15 years.

Dolphins: These mammals live anywhere from 3 to 5 years.

Goldfish: Goldfish live about 7 years on average.

Herrings: Pacific herring usually live to 8 years of age.

Minnows: Most varieties of the minnow live about 3 years.

Pike: Northern pike live about 10 years.

Salmon: Atlantic salmon live about 10 years and the sockeye salmon live about 8 years. The Pacific salmon's life expectancy is between 2 and 8 years.

Trout: The life span of a rainbow trout is about 7 to 11 years and a cutthroat trout lives about 6 to 9 years.

Walleyes: In southern states walleyes live about 6 to 7 years; in northern waters their life span doubles.

White bass: The average life span of a white bass is 3 to 4 years in warm waters and 4 to 5 years up north.

SOURCE: IBID.

Life Spans of Amphibians and Reptiles

Frogs: The common bullfrog and tree frog live up to 16 years.

Iguanas: These lizards live up to 25 years.

Lizards: The most common lizard kept in home terrariums is the anole, which has a life span of about 4 years.

Salamanders: Salamanders have a wide variety of life spans; many species live up to 25 years.

Snakes: Garter snakes live up to 6 to 10 years. Larger snakes like the cobra live up to 30 years.

Tortoises: There are many different kinds of tortoises, many of which live more than 100 years. SOURCE: IBID.

Animal Gestation Periods

Cat	63 days
Chimpanzee	226 days
Cow	280 days
Dog	61 days
Hamster	16–19 days
Horse	11 months
Pig	112–115 days

SOURCE: *THE HAMMOND ALMANAC*, 1983.

Life Span of Non-Fruit-Bearing Trees

Tree	Life Span
Southern poplar	100 years
Red maple	110
Dogwood	115
American holly	125
Pacific yew	200
Eastern black walnut	200
American elm	235
Shortleaf pine	235

Tree	Life Span
White fir	260 years
Sugar maple	275
Cascades fir	275
American beech	275
White ash	275
Red spruce	275
California cedar	350
Eastern hemlock	350
Red fir	350
Sugar pine	400
Ponderosa pine	450
White oak	450
Douglas fir	750
Redwood	1,000+
Giant sequoia	2,500+
Bristlecone pine	3,000+

SOURCE: AUTHORS' RESEARCH.

Life Span of Mammals

Mammal	Gestation	Sexual Maturity
Koala	About 1 month number of young: 1 time in pouch: 5–6 months	At about 3–4 years
Killer whale	13 months or more number of young: 1 every 2 years (capable of achieving some speeds of up to 30 mph (45 kmh) and beyond and of diving to depths of even longer than 20 minutes)	
Beaver	About 105 days number of young: 1–5, average 3	Usually at 3¾ years

Mammal	Gestation	Sexual Maturity
Wolf	60–62 days number of young: from 1–11, 5–6 on average	In second year
American black bear	About 7 months number of young: 2–3 (occasionally 1 or 4)	3½–5½ years
Leopard	90–105 days, average 96 number of young: 1–6 (average 2–3)	2–3 years
African elephant	20–22 months generally 1 young	?
Hippopotamus	240 days number of young: 1	Females at 9 years Males at 8 years
Camel	About 13 months number of young: 1	?
Giraffe	14–15½ months (about 450 days) number of young: 1–2	3 (5) years
Reindeer	About 7½–8 months number of young: 1, occasionally 2	Females at 2 years, males later
Indian buffalo	300–340 days number of young: 1	?
American bison	9 months number of young: 1	Females at 2 years, males much later
Black rhinoceros	16 months number of young: 1	5–6 years
Zebra	About 1 year number of young: 1	At 2–4 years
Gorilla	About 260 days number of young: 1	Female 6–7 years, male 8–10 years
Rocky Mountain goat	147–178 days number of young: 1, sometimes 2	Females at 2 years, males later
Sea otter	8–9 months number of young: 1	Not before 3 years

SOURCE: *GREAT BOOK OF THE ANIMAL KINGDOM*. ARCH CAPE PRESS (DISTRIBUTED BY CROWN PUBLISHERS), 1988.

Solid Waste

Every year, Americans generate about 150 million tons of municipal solid waste, or 3.5 pounds per person per day. According to the National Solid Wastes Management Association, 76 percent of that waste is currently landfilled, while only 11 percent is recycled and 13 percent is burned. Paper and paperboard constitute some 35 percent of the municipal solid waste stream. By the year 2000, less than half of the landfills existing today are expected to be operational—when 216 million tons of new garbage will need to be disposed of.

SOURCE: XEROX CORPORATION 1990 ANNUAL REPORT.

Recycling Paper

Wastepaper recycling makes economic as well as environmental sense; the practice saves 3 cubic yards of landfill, or about $50 in disposal costs, for every ton of recycled wastepaper. Compared to conventional paper manufactured from virgin fiber, every ton of recycled paper eliminates 60 pounds of air pollutants and saves 17 trees, 7,000 to 24,000 gallons of water, and 4,100 kilowatt hours of energy—enough to power a home for six months!

SOURCE: IBID.

Global Warming Warning

Those ozone-destroying chlorofluorocarbons are indeed making things warmer. A United Nations scientific panel concurred that a continued pumping of carbon dioxide and other greenhouse gases will warm the Earth at temperatures rising from 4 to 8 degrees F by the end of the next century, if emissions continue unchecked. While a few degrees doesn't seem like much, if temperatures change as much as 8 degrees, the planet would become warmer than it has been in millions of years. The difference between the ice ages and today is about 10 degrees.

SOURCE: MAURA DOLAN, "GLOBAL WARMING FORCES DECISIONS WITHOUT FACTS," *LOS ANGELES TIMES,* MARCH 29, 1992.

9. How Long Things Last

Old Planes

The average age of the nation's 3,671 commercial airliners is 13 years. SOURCE: FEDERAL AVIATION ADMINISTRATION.

Built to Last

A Boeing 747 is designed to fly 60,000 hours and to undergo 20,000 takeoff and landing cycles in 20 years. SOURCE: IBID.

American Marriages

The average American marriage lasts 9.4 years.

SOURCE: U.S. BUREAU OF THE CENSUS.

Extramarital Affairs

Women's extramarital affairs last, on average, 21 months. Men's last approximately 29 months.

SOURCE: TOM AND NANCY BIRACREE. *ALMANAC OF THE AMERICAN PEOPLE.* FACTS ON FILE, 1988.

Things That Last 1 Year

Socks
Aprons
Uniforms
Robes
Work shoes
Boys' shoes

SOURCE: INTERNATIONAL FABRICARE INSTITUTE.

Things That Last 2 Years

Bathing suits
Leather gloves
Men's dress shirts
Shorts
Sport coats
Suits
Underwear
Work clothes
Blouses
Negligees
Scarves
Women's shoes
Tablecloths
Bathroom towels

SOURCE: IBID.

Things That Last 3 Years

Raincoats
Wool or silk robes
Sweaters
Dress slacks
Bedspreads
Drapes
Sunlamp bulbs
Men's pajamas
Socks
Handkerchiefs

SOURCE: INSURANCE INFORMATION INSTITUTE.

Things That Last 4 Years

Men's coats and jackets
Wool pants

SOURCE: INSURANCE FABRICARE INSTITUTE.

Things That Last 5 Years

Tuxedos
Leather jackets
Lightweight and electric blankets

Interior paint job on house
Electric shavers
Mattress covers and pads
Pillowcases and sheets
Leather pocketbooks
Earrings, necklaces, and watches
Kitchen utensils
Lampshades
Typewriters
Wallets
Eyeglasses
Games, scooters, and tricycles
Washing machines*
Clothes dryers*

SOURCES: INSURANCE INFORMATION INSTITUTE AND U.S. CENSUS BUREAU(*).

Things That Last 6 Years

An exterior paint job
Dictation machines

SOURCE: INSURANCE INFORMATION INSTITUTE.

Things That last 7 Years

Clothes irons, including steam irons

SOURCE: IBID.

Things That Last 8 Years

Automatic washers

SOURCE: IBID.

Things That Last 10 Years

Fur coats*
Oil burners
Galvanized gutters
Room air conditioners
Dehumidifiers
Dishwashers
Stereos
Tape recorders
TV sets
Vacuum cleaners
Blenders
Coffeemakers
Heaters
Knife sharpeners
Roasters
Hair dryers
Toasters
Vaporizers
Bathroom scales
Mattresses
Baseball gloves
Bicycles
Camping equipment
Fishing tackle

Electric blankets
Can openers
Fans
Frying pans
Golf clubs
Outdoor motors
Calculators
Duplication machines

SOURCE: INSURANCE INFORMATION INSTITUTE AND INTERNATIONAL FABRICARE INSTITUTE(*).

Things That Last 15 Years

Air-conditioning systems over 5 tons
Gas furnaces
Asphalt roofs
Chest or upright freezers
Refrigerators
Space heaters
Kitchen stoves
Heating pads
Ironing boards
Sunlamps
Waffle irons
Wood furniture

SOURCE: INSURANCE INFORMATION INSTITUTE.

Things That Last 20 Years

Wiring in a home
Sewing machines
Quilts
Expensive clocks
High-quality cameras
Ladders
Suitcases
Mirrors
Bookcases
Desks
Pocketknives
Picture frames
Hand and power tools

SOURCE: IBID.

Things That Last a Quarter of a Century

Radiators
Asbestos roofs
Aluminum gutters
Barometers
Reference books
Firearms
Pianos

SOURCE: IBID.

Eggs

Fresh eggs will last at least 2 days at room temperature and about 10 days in the refrigerator. Hard-boiled eggs will keep up to 10 days in the refrigerator.

SOURCE: FRANK KENDIG AND RICHARD HUTTON. *LIFE-SPAN OR HOW LONG THINGS LAST.* HOLT, RINEHART AND WINSTON, 1979.

Nuts

Most nuts will remain fresh in their shell for 1 year. Vacuum-packed cans of nuts remain fresh for 1 year, unopened.

SOURCE: IBID.

Baked Goods

Breads and Rolls—Baked breads, muffins, rolls, and biscuits can be kept for 5 days at room temperature, 2 weeks in the refrigerator, and 3 to 6 months in the freezer.

Cakes and Cookies—Homemade cakes and cookies without fruit, nuts, fillings, and toppings can be kept for 1 to 2 weeks at room temperature or 6 months to a year in the freezer. Packaged cookies are protected with preservatives and will last up to 4 months at room temperature. Cakes and cookies with fruits and/or nuts will last up to 3 months at room temperature, 6 months in the refrigerator, and up to 1 year in the freezer.

Pies and Puddings—Fruit pies and baked custard pies can be kept for 2 to 4 days at room temperature, 3 to 7 days in the refrigerator, or 6 to 8 months in the freezer. Soft custard pies last only about 1 day at room temperature, 2 to 3 days in the refrigerator, and 2 months in the freezer.

SOURCE: IBID.

Refrigerating Tips (How Long Foods Last)

The following is a list of how long certain common foods last when stored in the refrigerator and can be served fresh:

Food	
Shell beans	2 to 3 days
Broccoli	3 to 4 days
Cabbage	2 days
Carrots	2 weeks
Cauliflower	4 days
Corn (unshucked)	1 day
Cucumbers	3 to 5 days
Eggplant	4 to 5 days
Leeks	5 days
Onions	5 days
Parsnips	3 weeks
Peas	4 days
Leafy green spinach	3 to 4 days
Squash (summer)	4 to 5 days
Zucchini	3 to 4 days

SOURCE: JULEE ROSSO AND SHEILA LUKINS. *THE NEW BASICS COOKBOOK.* WORKMAN PUBLISHING COMPANY, 1989.

The Deep Freeze

The following is a list of how long certain foods last when frozen at 0° F:

Meat, Fresh	
Beef, steaks or roasts	9 to 12 months
Beef, ground	4 to 6
Lamb	9 to 12
Pork	4 to 6
Pork, ground	1 to 3
Pork liver	1 to 2
Veal	9 to 12
Veal, ground	4 to 6
Meat, Smoked	
Bacon, slab (do not freeze sliced bacon)	1 to 3
Frankfurters	1 to 3
Ham, whole	1 to 3
Sausage	1 to 2

Poultry, Fresh	
Chicken, ready-to-cook	12 months
Ducks, geese, ready-to-cook	6
Fish and Shellfish	
Lean fish	4 to 6
Fatty fish, clams, oysters, scallops, raw shrimp	3 to 4
Cooked crabmeat and lobster meat	2 to 3
Cooked shrimp	1 to 2
Other Foods	
Butter and cheese, except cottage cheese (do not freeze cream cheese)	6 to 8
Fruits and vegetables	10 to 12
Ice Cream	1 to 2
Margarine	12
Cooked or Prepared Foods	
Baked pies, biscuits, muffins, waffles, cream puffs, sponge cake	2
Baked yeast breads and rolls	6 to 8
Cakes (frosted), loaves, doughnuts, pie and cookie dough, unbaked pies	4 to 6
Cakes (unfrosted), fruitcakes, unbaked fruit pies	6 to 8
Leftovers, fried foods, Newburgs, thermidors, pasta dishes	1
Roast beef, lamb, veal, and chicken, beans	4 to 6
Roast pork and turkey, stews, cooked vegetables, foods in sauces and gravy, chow mein, meat pies, meatballs and loaves, hash, gravies	2 to 4
Sandwiches	1 to 4 weeks
Soups	6 months
Turkey pies, stuffing, chili con carne	1 to 2 months
Unbaked biscuits, muffins	2 weeks
Unbaked yeast dough	2 weeks

SOURCE: *WOMAN'S DAY ENCYCLOPEDIA OF COOKERY*, VOL. 5, PUBLISHED BY *WOMAN'S DAY*, 1966.

Life Span of Fruit-Bearing Trees

Name of tree	Fruit-bearing age (years after transplanting)	Life span
Apple	3 to 5	25+ years
Apricot	2 to 3	12 to 15+
Cherry	2 to 3	20+
Grapevine	2 to 4	20
Nectarine	2 to 3	8 to 12
Peach	2 to 3	12+
Pear	4 to 5	25+
Plum	3 to 4	10 to 12

SOURCE: AUTHORS' RESEARCH.

Shelf Lives of Freeze-Dried Foods

	shelf life (months)		
Food	At 40° F	At 70° F	At 90° F
Steak	72	36	18
Chicken	72	36	18
Fish squares	72	36	18
Scrambled-egg mix	60	36	18
Apples and apple juice	72	36	18
Carrots	36	18	9
Cottage cheese	24	12	6
Cherries	48	24	12
Chives	24	12	6
Corn	48	12	6
Potato granules	72	36	18
Potato slices	36	18	9
Onions	48	24	12

SOURCE: FRANK KENDIG AND RICHARD HUTTON. *LIFE-SPANS OR HOW LONG THINGS LAST.* HOLT, RINEHART AND WINSTON, 1979.

Rolls-Royces Roll for a Long Time

It's estimated that more than half of all Rolls-Royce motorcars built since 1904 are still gliding along the road.

SOURCE: ROLLS-ROYCE.

Still Putting Along

About 25 million Model T Fords were made from 1908 to 1927, and dealers estimate that roughly 450,000 are still in running condition. Of the 4 million Model A's made from 1928 to 1931, at least 160,000 survive.

SOURCE: *WALL STREET JOURNAL*, MARCH 20, 1990.

Wasted Rubber

Most tires wear out 40,000 miles shy of their life span (80,000 to 100,000 miles). SOURCE: TIRE INDUSTRY SAFETY COUNCIL.

The Top 10 Most Popular Record Albums Since 1955

Album	Year Released	Weeks No. 1
1. *West Side Story* (soundtrack)	1962	54
2. *Thriller*, Michael Jackson	1983	37
3. *South Pacific* (soundtrack)	1958	31
4. *Calypso*, Harry Belafonte	1956	31
5. *Rumours*, Fleetwood Mac	1977	31
6. *Saturday Night Fever* (soundtrack)	1978	24
7. *Purple Rain*, Prince	1984	24
8. *Blue Hawaii*, Elvis Presley	1961	20
9. *More of the Monkees* (soundtrack)	1967	18
10. *Dirty Dancing* (soundtrack)	1988	18

SOURCES: *BILLBOARD;* RECORD RESEARCH, INC.

A Long Time on Prime Time

Here are the five television shows that lasted the longest on prime-time network TV:

	Seasons	Years
"The Ed Sullivan Show"	24	1948–71
"60 Minutes"	24	1968–Present
"Gunsmoke"	21	1955–75
"The Red Skelton Show"	21	1951–71
"What's My Line?"	18	1950–67

SOURCE: TIM BROOKS. *THE COMPLETE DIRECTORY TO PRIME-TIME NETWORK TV SHOWS.*

"Today" Is 40

On January 14, 1992, NBC's "Today" show celebrated its 40th anniversary. Since its first show in 1952, the show has logged an estimated 21,000 hours of air time.

SOURCE: "TODAY IS 40," AN NBC TELEVISION SPECIAL AIRED ON JANUARY 14, 1992.

10. Time and Money

Household Income

The median household income in 1988 was $27,230. For white households, median income was $28,780; for blacks it was $16,410, and for Hispanics it was $20,360.

SOURCE: U.S. CENSUS BUREAU

Married Couples Income

The median income for white married couples in 1988 was $36,840, for blacks it was $30,385, and for Hispanics it was $25,667.

SOURCE: IBID.

Cost of Getting Along

The average American family needs $419 a week to meet expenses. This weekly figure translates to $21,800 a year. Residents of New England and the West Coast report the highest cost of living—$24,500 a year in New England and $24,400 in the Pacific states. The lowest cost of living is in the Southwest or Rocky Mountain states, averaging about $19,800. People living in suburbs say they need $23,300 to get along and people in nonmetropolitan areas say that it takes only $17,500 a year to survive.

SOURCE: THE GALLUP ORGANIZATION, MAY 1989 POLL OF 1,073 ADULTS.

Baseball Salaries

The average baseball salary on opening day 1991 was $891,188. Oakland led, with a payroll of $36,432,500, and an average salary of $1,349,352. New York Mets had the second highest average payroll at $1,251,538 and Los Angeles was third with a payroll of $1,248,212. Houston had the lowest average at $487,090. SOURCE: MAJOR LEAGUE BASEBALL PLAYERS ASSOCIATION.

Little Kids' Income

Chilren's income averages $4.42 a week, or $229.84 a year. These 4- to 12-year-olds spend $159.64 of this and save $70.20 a year. 4-year-olds spend just 83¢ a week, six-year-olds spend $2.59, and 12-year-olds spend $6.90 a week.

SOURCE: *AMERICAN DEMOGRAPHICS*, SEPTEMBER 1990.

Eating Your Money Away

The average annual amount spent for food in households under the age of 35 is $3,347. For households age 35 to 44 it is $4,721, 45 to 54 it's $4,885, 55 to 64 it's $3,983, and for households 65 and older $2,708 is spent on food each year.

SOURCE: BUREAU OF LABOR STATISTICS, COMBINED 1987 TO 1988 INTEGRATED CONSUMER EXPENDITURE SURVEY.

Money Spent on Particular Foods

In 1988 American households spent the following amounts on certain foods:

Cereals and bakery products	$312
Meats, poultry, fish, and eggs	$551
Dairy products	$274
Fruits and vegetables	$373

SOURCE: AVERAGE ANNUAL EXPENDITURES FROM BUREAU OF LABOR STATISTICS.

Department Store Shoppers

The average customer spends $100 a month at department stores. The average 55- to 64-year-old spends $89, and the average person 65 or older spends just $53. But 25- to 34-year-olds spend $108, 35- to 44-year-olds spend $126, and 45- to 54-year-olds spend $116. SOURCE: MARVIN J. ROTHENBERG, INC., FAIR LAWN, NJ.

Money Spent on Women's Apparel

The average households spends $492 a year on women's apparel. SOURCE: AVERAGE ANNUAL EXPENDITURES FROM BUREAU OF LABOR STATISTICS; AUTHORS' INDEX.

Money Spent on Men's Apparel

The average household spends $311 a year on men's apparel.
SOURCE: IBID.

Infants' Clothing

Households under age 25 spend an average of $59 a year on infants' clothing. Households ages 25 to 34 spend $123 a year on children's clothing, households ages 35 to 44 spend $67 a year, and households ages 45 and older spend $32 a year.
SOURCE: BUREAU OF LABOR STATISTICS, CONSUMER EXPENDITURE SURVEY, 1988.

Money Spent on Boys' Clothing

Households under age 25 spend an average of $14 each year on boys' clothing, households ages 25 to 34 spend $66 a year, households ages 34 to 44 spend $137 a year, and households ages 45 and older spend $28 a year. SOURCE: IBID.

Money Spent on Girls' Clothing

Households under age 25 spend an average of $12 each year on girls' clothing, households ages 25 to 34 spend $84 a year, households ages 35 to 44 spend $170 a year, and households ages 45 and older spend $39 a year. SOURCE: IBID.

Health Care Costs

The average American household spends $1,298 a year on health care costs: $474 for health care insurance, $529 for medical services, $223 for drugs, and $71 for medical supplies.
SOURCE: AVERAGE ANNUAL EXPENDITURES FROM BUREAU OF LABOR STATISTICS.

Gift Spending

The average household spends $680 on gifts each year. Households under age 25 average $283, whereas households ages 45 to 54 average $1,083 a year on gifts. SOURCE: IBID.

Giving Grandparents

In 1990 grandparents spent an average of $250 a year on their grandchildren. SOURCE: ROPER REPORTS.

Garden Expenses

Eastern and Western gardeners spend a household average of $259 and $291 a year, respectively, on garden-related expenses. Midwesterners spend $232 per household and households in the South average only $215 a year on gardening.
SOURCE: *AMERICAN DEMOGRAPHICS*, JULY 1990.

Out for Lunch

The average American households spend $9.10 a week on lunch eaten away from home, or about $473 a year. Households with annual incomes of $50,000 or more spend $18.66 a week, or about $970 a year going out to lunches.

SOURCE: BUREAU OF LABOR STATISTICS.

Visitors' Spending

1989 was the first year when spending by visitors ($43 billion) exceeded the spending of American travelers outside U.S. borders ($42.6 billion). Overseas guests spend an average of 20 nights in the States. Each visitor spends about $1,480 in the States, or about $74 a day. They spend a total of $2,388 per person and $3,820 for each travel party in the United States, including airfare. SOURCE: U.S. TRAVEL AND TOURISM ADMINISTRATION.

Happy Birthday to Fido

40 percent of American dog owners celebrate their pet's birthday every year. SOURCE: NATIONAL DOG REGISTRY.

Money Spent on Toys

Households under age 25 spend an average of $40 a year on toys, games, hobbies, and tricycles, households ages 25 to 34 spend $140 a year, households ages 35 to 44 spend $147 a year, and households ages 45 and older spend an average of $65 a year.

SOURCE: BUREAU OF LABOR STATISTICS, CONSUMER EXPENDITURE SURVEY, 1988.

Personal Insurance and Pensions

The average American living in a rural area spends an average of $1,880 on personal insurance and pensions each year, whereas the average urbanite spends $2,569 a year.

SOURCE: BUREAU OF LABOR STATISTICS, CONSUMER EXPENDITURE SURVEY, 1989.

Money Spent on Reading Materials

The average household with a college education spends an average of $195 a year on reading materials, whereas the household without a college education spends $99 a year on these materials.

SOURCE: IBID.

Annual Furniture Expenses

Households under the age of 35 spend an average of $310 a year on furniture, the 35 to 44 group spends an average of $443, 45 to 54 spend $426, 55 to 64 spend $316, and households ages 65 and older spend an average of $128 a year on furniture.

SOURCE: BUREAU OF LABOR STATISTICS, COMBINED 1987–88 CONSUMER EXPENDITURE SURVEY.

Phone Bills

The average homeowner spends $600 a year on phone service.

SOURCE: SIMMONS MARKET RESEARCH BUREAU, SPRING 1989.

Additional Purchases for New Homeowners

New homeowners plan to spend an average of $4,700 on new furniture and accessories and $2,200 on appliances during their first year of home ownership.

SOURCE: BUREAU OF LABOR STATISTICS, CONSUMER EXPENDITURE SURVEY, 1988.

Closing Costs

The first expense in home ownership is closing costs, which averaged $8,000 in 1988, including the down payment, mortgage "points," legal fees, and insurance deposits.

SOURCE: IBID.

Financing Your House

At 10 percent, a 15-year $100,000 house mortgage will require monthly payments of $1,075. During the period that the loan is outstanding, the total payback will be $193,430. If the house is financed for 25 years at the same rate of interest, the monthly payments are $909 for a total payback of $218,090; at 30 years, the monthly payments of $878 will total $315,929.

Although the monthly payments of $909 differ by only $166, the 25-year mortgage will cost nearly $25,000 more in total payments than the 15-year mortgage. The monthly payments of $878 are reduced by $197, with the 30-year loan, but during the course of the full period, with interest compounded annually, the borrower will pay a total of $315,929, or an additional $122,500 as compared with the 15-year mortgage.

At 12 percent, the difference between the total payments of a 15-year $100,000 house mortgage and the 30-year mortgage is $154,273. When these figures are doubled and tripled for $200,000 and $300,000, the compound interest really adds up!

SOURCE: AUTHORS' CALCULATIONS.

Urban vs. Rural Costs of Housing

	Annual Spending in 1989	
	Rural	**Urban**
Housing	$6,277	$8,993
Shelter	2,821	5,166
Utilities, fuel, public services	1,837	1,834
Household operations	300	486
Housekeeping supplies	352	401
Furnishings and equipment	967	1,106

SOURCE: BUREAU OF LABOR STATISTICS, CONSUMER EXPENDITURE SURVEY, 1989.

Single Entertainment

Women who live alone spend an average of $569 a year on entertainment, compared with $1,019 for men. Single women spend an average of $182 on fees and admissions (show tickets, etc.), whereas single men spend an average of $295. Women spend an average of $194 on TVs and other electronic equipment, whereas men spend $345.

SOURCE: IBID.

Annual Transportation Costs in 1989

	Rural	Urban
Purchase of vehicle for one year	$2,429	$2,268
Gas and oil	1,168	955
Other vehicle expenses	1,402	1,665
Public transportation	128	309

SOURCE: IBID.

Smoking Expenses

In 1989 the average American living in rural areas spent an average of $272 a year on tobacco and supplies, whereas the average urbanite spent $259 a year on these items.

SOURCE: IBID.

Food and Beverages

The average American household spent $4,017 on food and alcoholic beverages in 1988. This amounted to about 16 percent of the total household budget.

SOURCE: IBID.

Meat Eaters

The average urban U.S. household spent $445 on beef, pork, poultry, and seafood consumed in the home in 1987, down from $488 in 1980.

SOURCE: BUREAU OF LABOR STATISTICS, CONSUMER EXPENDITURE SURVEY, 1987.

An Expensive First Year

In 1989, a baby cost an average of $5,774 in its first year of life. Here's the breakdown:

Food and feeding equipment	$ 855
Diapers	570
Clothes	352
Furniture	995
Bedding and bath supplies	223
Medicine (vitamins and personal care products)	396
Toys	199
Day care	2,184

SOURCE: U.S. BUREAU OF THE CENSUS, NATIONAL CENTER FOR HEALTH STATISTICS, U.S. DEPARTMENT OF AGRICULTURE.

18 Years of Expenses

The average cost of raising a child from birth to age 18 is about $100,000. SOURCE: U.S. DEPARTMENT OF AGRICULTURE.

The High Cost of Teenage Childbearing

In 1988, the United States spent nearly $20 billion in welfare payments and other benefits on families headed by teenage mothers. The 364,587 such families begun in 1988 will cost $6 billion over 20 years. If those births had been delayed by only a few years, the savings would have been about $2 billion.

SOURCE: CENTER FOR POPULATION OPTIONS.

The Cost of a Mortgage

Monthly principal, interest per $1,000 mortgage.

Mortgage Rate	15-Year Loan	20-Year Loan	25-Year Loan	30-Year Loan
8	9.56	8.37	7.72	7.34
8¼	9.71	8.53	7.89	7.52
8½	9.85	8.68	8.06	7.69
8¾	10.00	8.84	8.23	7.87

Mortgage Rate	15-Year Loan	20-Year Loan	25-Year Loan	30-Year Loan
9	10.15	9.00	8.40	8.05
9¼	10.30	9.16	8.57	8.23
9½	10.45	9.33	8.74	8.41
9¾	10.60	9.49	8.92	8.60
10	10.75	9.66	9.09	8.78
10¼	10.90	9.82	9.27	8.97
10½	11.06	9.99	9.45	9.15
10¾	11.21	10.16	9.63	9.34
11	11.37	10.33	9.81	9.53
11¼	11.53	10.50	9.99	9.72
11½	11.69	10.67	10.17	9.91
11¾	11.85	10.84	10.35	10.10
12	12.01	11.02	10.54	10.29
12¼	12.17	11.19	10.72	10.46
12½	12.33	11.37	10.91	10.68
12¾	12.49	11.54	11.10	10.87
13	12.66	11.72	11.28	11.07
13¼	12.82	11.90	11.47	11.25
13½	12.99	12.08	11.66	11.46
13¾	13.15	12.26	11.85	11.66
14	13.32	12.44	12.04	11.85
14¼	13.49	12.62	12.23	12.05
14½	13.66	12.80	12.43	12.25
14¾	13.83	12.99	12.62	12.45
15	14.00	13.17	12.81	12.65
15½	14.34	13.54	13.20	13.05

Note: Multiply the cost per $1,000 by the size of the mortgage (in thousands). The result is the monthly payment, including principal and interest. For example, for a $48,500 mortgage for 30 years at 13 percent, multiply 48.5 × 11.07 = $536.90.

SOURCE: CHICAGO TITLE INSURANCE CO.

Mortgage Payments

A $200,000 mortgage will have the following payments based on interest at 10 and 12 percent.

Interest	Length of Mortgage	Monthly Payments	Total Payments
10%	15 years	$2,149.30	$386,687
10%	25 years	$1,817.50	$545,250
10%	30 years	$1,719.40	$618,912
12%	15 years	$2,400.40	$432,072
12%	25 years	$2,106.50	$631,959
12%	30 years	$2,057.30	$740,618

Observe, for example, that your monthly payments on a 15-year $200,000 mortgage at 12 percent are $2,400.40, or $343.10 more than a 30-year mortgage. If you are willing to stretch your monthly payments by $343.10, however, you will pay $318,546 less during the duration of the loan in comparison with a 30-year mortgage. Or look at it this way: a 15-year loan taken out at age 50 means that there are no more monthly payments after you reach age 65. On a 30-year mortgage, however, you are obligated to continue making monthly payments in the amount of $2,057.30 until you are 80 years old! SOURCE: AUTHORS' CALCULATIONS.

Keeping Up with Inflation

Assuming a modest 4.5 percent inflation rate and a life span of 90 years, a 65-year-old retiring today must nearly triple his or her income over the next 20 years just to stay even.

SOURCE: *WALL STREET JOURNAL*, NOVEMBER 13, 1990.

The Amazing Rule of 72

To use the Rule of 72, divide 72 by the interest rate you receive on a particular investment to arrive at the number of years it will take the investment to double. For example, if you invest $10,000 at 10 percent compound interest, then according to Rule of 72, in 7.2 years (72 divided by 10) your money will double to $20,000. Let's say you decide not to invest your $20,000 but to hide it in your drawer instead. Assuming a 9 percent inflation rate, in 8 years (72 divided by 9) the value of your $10,000 will be halved.

SOURCE: B. O'NEILL WYSS, "DOLLARS & SENSE," *TWA AMBASSADOR,* APRIL 1991.

Plastic Addicts

Every day more than 200 million credit cards slide in and out of charge machines across the United States. $480 billion was charged in 1990, at a rate of about $1 million per minute. On average, American Express card members charge $4,266 per card every year versus $1,577 among bank cardholders.

SOURCE: AUTHORS' CALCULATIONS BASED ON ARTICLE BY JANICE CASTRO, "CHARGE IT YOUR WAY," *TIME*, JULY 1, 1991, P. 50.

Investment Phone Scams

Investment phone scams cost American consumers some $10 billion per year—that's more than $1 million an hour.

SOURCE: NORTH AMERICAN SECURITIES ADMINISTRATORS ADMINISTRATION.

Starting Pay for Engineers

The average salary for an engineer with a bachelor's degree was $45,000 in 1990.

SOURCE: COMMISSION OF PROFESSIONALS IN SCIENCE AND TECHNOLOGY.

Higher the Degree, Higher the Earnings

In 1987, monthly earnings for:

High-school graduates with no college education	$ 921
Some college but no degree or vocational degrees	$1,088
Associate's degree	$1,458
Bachelor's degree	$1,829
Master's degree	$2,378
Ph.D.	$3,637
Professional degrees (Fields such as law and medicine)	$4,003

SOUCE: U.S. CENSUS BUREAU.

Grand Grand Larceny

It's reported that the late President Ferdinand Marcos and his wife Imelda stole as much as $10 billion during their 20-year rule of the Philippines. That amounts to taking $1,369,863 out of the till every day for 20 consecutive years!

SOURCE: AUTHORS' CALCULATIONS.

Male Lawyers Earn More

For every dollar earned by male lawyers, female lawyers earn 63 cents.

SOURCE: TOM AND NANCY BIRACREE. *ALMANAC OF THE AMERICAN PEOPLE*. FACTS ON FILE, 1988.

Wives Earn Less

On average, wives' earnings are 45 percent of their husbands' earnings.

SOURCE: *CENSUS AND YOU: MONTHLY NEWS FROM THE U.S. BUREAU OF THE CENSUS*, OCTOBER 1989.

Males Donate More

Females donate an average of $360 a year (1.4 percent of their income) to charitable organizations, whereas males donate $590 a year (1.8 percent of income).

SOURCE: "AMERICANS AND THEIR MONEY," *MONEY MAGAZINE*, 1988.

Pooling Resources

66 percent of wives and 74 percent of husbands married 2 to 10 years favor pooling resources. 40 percent of lesbians and 44 percent of gay men together 2 to 10 years favor pooling their resources.

SOURCE: PHILIP BLUMSTEIN AND PEPPER SCHWARTZ. *AMERICAN COUPLES*. POCKET BOOKS, 1985.

Buying and Selling Stocks

3 percent of females and 7 percent of males have bought stocks in the past month. 2 percent of females and 4 percent of males have sold stocks in the last month.

SOURCE: *ROPER REPORTS*, JULY 1989.

Income Tax Returns

82 percent of females and 89 percent of males filed federal income tax returns this year.

SOURCE: "AMERICANS AND THEIR MONEY," *MONEY MAGAZINE*, 1988.

Dollars for Day Care

Working parents in Boston pay nearly 3 times as much for day care as their peers in Ogden, Utah.

Here are the 10 most expensive and the 10 least expensive metropolitan areas for weekly day-care costs in 1990:

Most Expensive		Least Expensive	
1. Boston, MA	$109	1. Ogden, UT	$38
2. New York, NY	95	2. Mobile, AL	42
3. Anchorage, AK	91	3. Jackson, MS	44
4. Manchester, NH	90	4. Huntington, WV	45
5. Washington, DC	87	5. Columbia, SC	46
6. Minneapolis, MN	87	6. Boise, ID	46
7. Hartford, CT	86	7. Cheyenne, WY	48
8. Philadelphia, PA	86	8. Little Rock, AR	50
9. Portland, ME	83	9. Grand Island, NE	51
10. Burlington, VT	79	10. Tucson, AZ	51

Note: Costs are based on a 3-year-old who spends 40 hours a week in a for-profit day-care center in a suburban community surrounding the central city.

SOURCE: RUNSHEIMER INTERNATIONAL, ROCHESTER, WISCONSIN.

Party Towns

7 of the 10 hardest-drinking metropolitan areas in the United States are ports. (Average annual spending on alcoholic beverages per household, dollar amount and index, 1987–1988.

		Index (%)
U.S. Average	**$279**	**100**
1. Miami	546	196
2. Anchorage	531	190
3. San Diego	465	167
4. Seattle	456	163
5. Boston	441	158
6. Washington, DC	422	151
7. San Francisco	413	148
8. Baltimore	405	145
9. Milwaukee	390	140
10. Dallas-Fort Worth	377	135
11. Detroit	373	134
12. Houston	371	133
13. Philadelphia	362	130
14. Chicago	344	123
15. Los Angeles	338	121
16. Minneapolis-St. Paul	335	120
17. Honolulu	329	118
18. Portland, OR	328	118
19. New York	318	114
20. Cleveland	286	103
21. Buffalo	284	102
22. Kansas City	277	99
23. Cincinnati	239	86
24. St. Louis	239	86
25. Pittsburgh	215	77
26. Atlanta	200	72

SOURCE: BUREAU OF LABOR STATISTICS, COMBINED 1987–1988 CONSUMER EXPENDITURES SURVEY.

For Your Convenience

The average purchase per customer in a convenience store is $2.29. SOURCE: NATIONAL ASSOCIATION OF CONVENIENCE STORES, 1990.

Top Paid Entertainers

1. Bill Cosby—In 1989 and 1990 Bill Cosby's total income was $115 million. Assuming Bill works 50 weeks per year, he earns $1,150,000 each week. Working 40 hours a week this comes out to $28,750 an hour, or about $480 a minute, which is $8 a second.

2. Michael Jackson—In 1989 and 1990 Michael Jackson's income totaled $100 million.

3. The Rolling Stones—The Stones earned $88 million in 1989 and 1990. In North America alone, more than 3 million fans paid a total of $98 million to see their Steel Wheels concert.

4. Steven Spielberg—Producer-director Spielberg earned $87 million in 1989 and 1990.

5. New Kids On The Block—These 5 youngsters earned a 2-year total income of $78 million. Columbia Records sold more than 20 million New Kids records in 2 years.

6. Oprah Winfrey—Oprah's 2-year income totaled $68 million. This 38-year-old talk-show queen is seen in 198 television markets and 12 foreign countries.

7. Sylvester Stallone—Stallone, 46, earned a 2-year total income of $63 million in 1989 and 1990. He now earns $25 million per movie.

8. Madonna—Madonna's 2-year total income in 1989 and 1990 was $62 million.

9. Arnold Schwarzenegger—Arnold's 2-year total income in 1989 and 1990 was $55 million. He received an estimated $15 million for his lead in *Terminator 2*.

10. Charles M. Schulz—Schulz's "Peanuts" remains the world's number 1 comic strip. The Peanuts characters earned $54 million for Charles in 1989 and 1990.

SOURCE: *FORBES*, OCTOBER 1, 1990.

Public Debt of the United States

In 1989 the U.S. debt was $2,857 billion, which averages out to be $11,545 per person. The U.S. paid $240.8 billion in interest in 1989.

SOURCE: U.S. TREASURY DEPARTMENT, BUREAU OF PUBLIC DEBT.

Investment Abroad

In 1989 the United States invested $373,436 billion abroad in various countries.

SOURCE: BUREAU OF ECONOMIC ANALYSIS, U.S. COMMERCE DEPARTMENT.

Bank Failures

In 1980, there were 10 bank failures; in 1985 there were 120; and in 1989 there were 206.

SOURCE: FEDERAL DEPOSIT INSURANCE CORPORATION.

Domestic Coin Production

In 1989 the domestic coin production was:

Pennies	12,837,140,268
Nickels	1,497,523,652
Dimes	2,240,355,488
Quarters	1,417,290,422
Half-dollars	41,196,188
Total	18,033,506,018

SOURCE: UNITED STATES MINT, U.S. TREASURY DEPARTMENT.

Which Do You Choose?

Take your choice: you may select to receive (1) $1 million or (2) beginning with $1 on day 1, double your money every succeeding day for a month of 31 days. If given the choice, take number 2. Here's why:

Day	Dollar Amount	Day	Dollar Amount
1	$ 1	17	$ 65,536
2	2	18	131,072
3	4	19	262,144
4	8	20	524,288
5	16	21	1,048,576
6	32	22	2,097,152
7	64	23	4,194,304
8	128	24	8,388,608
9	256	25	16,777,216
10	512	26	33,554,432
11	1,024	27	67,108,854
12	2,048	28	134,217,728
13	4,096	29	268,435,456
14	8,192	30	536,870,912
15	16,384	31	1,073,741,824
16	32,768		

SOURCE: AUTHORS' CALCULATIONS.

Time Payment Plan vs. Revolving Charge Plan

Here are two different cases to help you understand the difference in interest costs:

Case A: You borrow $300 for 1 year at 18 percent interest. If you pay the entire amount in 12 monthly installments, at the end of the year you will have paid $354.

Case B: You borrow $300 on a revolving charge with 18 percent interest and make 12 monthly payments; interest is charged only on the money owed (the unpaid balance).

When money is borrowed on a time payment contract, as in Case A, and 18 percent of the total amount financed is added to the unpaid balance and divided by 12, it looks like this:

Time Payment Plan (A)

$300.00 (amount financed)
+ 4.50 (interest paid in January)
+ 4.50 (interest paid in February)

+ 4.50 (interest paid in March)
+ 4.50 (interest paid in April)
+ 4.50 (interest paid in May)
+ 4.50 (interest paid in June)
+ 4.50 (interest paid in July)
+ 4.50 (interest paid in August)
+ 4.50 (interest paid in September)
+ 4.50 (interest paid in October)
+ 4.50 (interest paid in November)
+ 4.50 (interest paid in December)

$54.00 (total interest paid plus $25 per month for a total of $354)

However, if the interest is charged only on the current balance as in Case B above, it looks like this:

Revolving Charge Plan (B)

$300 (amount financed)
+ 4.50 (amount paid in January)
+ 4.12 (amount paid in February)
+ 3.75 (amount paid in March)
+ 3.37 (amount paid in April)
+ 3.00 (amount paid in May)
+ 2.62 (amount paid in June)
+ 2.25 (amount paid in July)
+ 1.87 (amount paid in August)
+ 1.50 (amount paid in September)
+ 1.12 (amount paid in October)
+ .75 (amount paid in November)
+ .37 (amount paid in December)

$29.22 (total interest paid, plus $25 per month for a total of $329.72)

The interest is figured only on the amount remaining to be repaid each month and therefore it decreases with each payment.

In Case A you will have paid $24.78 more interest than in Case B. If you carried $1,000 at 18 percent on a revolving charge, you would pay $195 on a 2-year payout compared with $360 on a 2-year time-payment contract—a total savings of $165.

It should be noted that had you borrowed $300 and paid

back the entire sum at the end of the year without having made any monthly payments of principal and interest, you would have paid an interest rate of 18 percent for a total of $354. However, on the time-payment plan, since you were paying $4.50 interest each month on the remaining balance, you were actually paying 36 percent interest. For example, in January, you paid 18 percent on an annual basis, which was $4.50 on the full amount of $300 that was borrowed. In July, you continued to pay $4.50, but the remaining balance was only $250, which means you were actually paying an annual interest rate of 36 percent ($150 × 36% = $54. When $54 is divided by 12, it equals $4.50). The monthly interest on $150 at 18 percent is $2.25. Similarly, when the balance is only $25 during the final month, you are still paying $4.50, which, on an annualized basis, is 216 percent. The interest rate of 18 percent on $25 is only 37 cents on a monthly basis!

Once you know the above, it is obvious that you must be sure to avoid making a loan that has anything to do with a time-payment plan. Our advice is to shop around for a better loan.

SOURCE: AUTHORS' CALCULATIONS.

Who Says the Indians Got Cheated When They Sold Manhattan to the Dutch for $24!

At an interest rate of 8 percent based on the Rule of 72, the $24 that the Indians received for Manhattan in 1624, would have doubled with compound interest every 9 years and today would be worth far more than the combined total of all the real estate on the island of Manhattan. By the year 1993, it would have been worth more than $52 trillion!

Year	Amount (in dollars)
1624	$ 24.
1633	48.
1642	96.
1651	192.

Year	Amount (in dollars)
1660	384.
1669	768.
1678	1,536.
1687	3,072.
1696	6,144.
1705	12,288.
1714	24,576.
1723	49,152.
1732	98.304.
1741	196,608.
1750	393,216.
1759	786.432.
1768	1,572.864.
1777	3,145,720.
1786	6,291,456.
1795	12,582,912.
1804	25,165,824.
1813	50,331,648.
1822	100,663,296.
1831	201,326,592.
1840	402,653,184.
1849	805,306,368.
1858	1,610,612,736.
1867	3,221,225,472.
1876	6,442,450,944.
1885	12,884,901,888.
1894	25,769,803,776.
1903	51,539,607,552.
1912	103,079,215,104.
1921	206,158,840,208.
1930	412,316,860,416.
1939	824,633,720,832.
1948	1,649,267,441,660.
1957	3,298,534,883,320.
1966	6,597,069,766,640.
1975	13,194,139,533,280.
1984	26,388,279,066,560.
1993	$52,776,548,133,120.

SOURCE: AUTHORS' CALCULATIONS.

Starting Salaries

The average starting salary for a college graduate with a bachelor's degree is $25,256, with an MBA the starting salary is $39,840. The highest starting salary is in engineering, with an average of $33,380 for chemical engineers, $32,256 for mechanical engineers, and $32,107 for electrical engineers.

USA TODAY, DECEMBER 11, 1989.

Auto Premiums

The average annual cost of an auto insurance premium in the United States was $517.71 in 1988.

The states with the lowest premiums are:

Alabama	$278.33
Iowa	$292.51
South Dakota	$324.90
Tennessee	$338.46
North Dakota	$343.85

SOURCE: A. M. BEST CO.

Car Phones

The average monthly cellular phone bill for the 4.4 million car phones in the United States for the first 6 months of 1990 was $89.30. The average length of calls was 2.3 minutes.

SOURCE: CELLULAR TELECOMMUNICATIONS INDUSTRY ASSOCIATION.

Average NFL Pay

The National Football League has 1,372 players who make an average of about $250,000 per year. SOURCE: NFL.

Paid by the Hour

59 percent of American workers are paid by the hour.

SOURCE: *STATISTICAL ABSTRACT OF THE UNITED STATES 1987*. BUREAU OF THE CENSUS. U.S. DEPARTMENT OF COMMERCE.

Principals' Salaries

The average high-school principal earns $55,722 each year; the salary for a junior-high-school principal averages $52,163, and the average is $48,431 for elementary principals.

SOURCE: THE NATIONAL ASSOCIATION OF SECONDARY SCHOOL PRINCIPALS.

Teachers' Pay

Teachers in the United States had an average salary of about $21,178 in the 1990 to 1991 school year.

Above average:

Far West	$35,310
Mid-Atlantic region	34,689
New England	33,964
Great Lakes states	33,425

Pay is below average in:

Southwest	26,355
Southeast	26,883
Mountain states	27,542
Plains states	27,874

SOURCE: EDUCATIONAL RESEARCH SERVICE.

Spending a Billion

It takes a lot of hard work to spend a billion dollars. Based on a 40-hour "work" week and $1 billion, one would have to spend $500,000 an hour, or at the rate of $8,333.33 per minute in order to deplete his or her wealth in a year's time.

In 1991, there were 274 billionaires in the world who could afford such spending habits.

SOURCE: AUTHORS' CALCULATIONS AND HAROLD SENECKER, ED., "THE WORLD'S BILLIONAIRES," *FORBES*, JULY 22, 1991. P. 98.

America's Richest Person

The net worth of John Werner Kluge, CEO of Metromedia, was $5.6 billion in 1991. To accumulate this amount of wealth, one would have to earn more than $100 million after taxes each year for 50 years. SOURCE: AUTHORS' CALCULATIONS.

America's Billionaires

In 1991, there were 32 billionaires in the United States versus 37 in 1990. SOURCE: HAROLD SENECKER, ED., "THE WORLD'S BILLIONAIRES," *FORBES*, JULY 22, 1991, P. 126.

Bill It to the Billionaires

If the total net worths of America's 32 billionaires (which totaled $207 billion in 1991) were donated to the U.S. government, it would be enough to keep the nation afloat for about 2 months. SOURCE: IBID.

The Plight of the Under-30 Generation

Measured in inflation-adjusted dollars, the median income of families headed by someone under age 30 in 1991 was 13 percent lower than such families earned in 1973.

SOURCE: NORTHEASTERN UNIVERSITY CENTER FOR LABOR MARKET STUDIES.

Steady Work Hard to Find for High-School Dropouts

In 1973, a majority of high-school dropouts had found steady work by age 22. In 1991, it takes until about age 26. In any given year, about 1 in 10 males aged 18 to 29 earns nothing—up 40 percent since 1973. SOURCE: U.S. CENSUS BUREAU.

Coffee Expenditures

In 1989, Americans drank more than 368 million cups of coffee a day. Here are the areas where households spent the most annually on their coffee:

Pittsburgh, PA	$88.03
Portland, ME	$66.14
Albany, NY	$63.68
Hartford, CT	$63.62
Scranton, PA	$58.06
Buffalo, NY	$57.39
Portland, OR	$57.37
Grand Rapids, MI	$56.41
Boston, MA	$55.93
Charleston, WV	$55.02

SOURCE: NATIONAL COFFEE ASSOCIATION OF AMERICA.

High Cost to Run a Car

Depending on the size of the vehicle you drive, the yearly cost to own and operate a 1991 vehicle ranged from $3,580 for a subcompact to $5,559 for a full-size car. For example, a subcompact such as the 1991 Ford Escort cost about 35.83 cents a mile to own and operate, and midsize cars like the 1991 Ford Taurus averaged 43.64 cents a mile. The owner of a full-size car such as the 1991 Chevy Caprice spent 55.59 cents a mile.

SOURCE: AMERICAN AUTOMOBILE ASSOCIATION.

Pump It Yourself

In 1989, the average car consumed 498 gallons of gas. The average price for full-service gas was $1.26 and $1.04 for self-serve. Based on these numbers, pumping your own gas in 1989 saved $109.56.

SOURCE: RUNZHEIMER INTERNATIONAL AND FEDERAL HIGHWAY ADMINISTRATION.

Governor Salaries

The 50 state governors earn an average annual salary of $79,800. The highest paid is New York Governor Mario Cuomo, who earned about $130,000 in 1991. The lowest paid is Governor Bill Clinton of Arkansas who received only $35,000 in 1991. SOURCE: *GOVERNING MAGAZINE*.

Living Off a Billion

$1 billion, if put into a long-term tax-free municipal bond at 7 percent interest, would earn $191,780 a day. That same amount, earning 6 percent interest in a shorter-term taxable account, would generate $164,383 each day, except that the IRS's share would be about $50,000. SOURCE: AUTHORS' CALCULATIONS.

Franchised Businesses Bring in the Bucks

In 1989, franchises in the United States earned more than $678 billion in sales. SOURCE: INTERNATIONAL FRANCHISE ASSOCIATION.

Trying Your Luck

On average, residents spent the following amounts on lottery tickets for the entire year in 1988:

Massachusetts	$235	Pennsylvania	$121
District of Columbia	$197	Illinois	$113
Maryland	$185	Delaware	$89
Connecticut	$162	New York	$88
New Jersey	$155	California	$80
Michigan	$132	New Hampshire	$73
Ohio	$128	Maine	$71

Vermont	$66	South Dakota	$37
Rhode Island	$63	Montana	$32
Oregon	$60	Missouri	$29
Arizona	$54	West Virginia	$29
Florida	$54	Colorado	$28
Washington	$49	Kansas	$27
Iowa	$43		

SOURCE: *U.S. NEWS & WORLD REPORT*, MAY 22, 1989.

Household Incomes

In 1989, 22 million U.S. households, or 23 percent, had total incomes of $50,000 or more. Only 13 percent of the 31 million one-earner households had incomes of $50,000 or more. Of the 33 million dual-earner households, 35 percent had incomes in excess of $50,000. Annual earnings over $50,000 is what many marketing specialists consider the threshold of affluence.

SOURCE: U.S. CENSUS BUREAU.

The $160 Billion Savings and Loan Bailout

If a company was capitalized with $1 billion in the year 1, and it lost $1,000 each day, it would still be in business today, 2,000 years later. In fact, it would take another 800 years until it ran out of money. That's with a billion dollars! So, it will take $160,000 a day for the next 2,800 years to pay back the $160 billion that was lost by the savings and loan institutions in the United States. Of course, we could speed those payments up and pay it off in 100 years. This would require $4,480,000 every day for the next century.

SOURCE: AUTHORS' CALCULATIONS.

The High Cost of Education in 2006

A conservative estimate of the cost of 4 years at a public university 15 years from now is $100,000. Assuming your investments are able to keep pace with the rate at which college costs are rising, earning 8 percent after taxes, it would still take a lump-sum investment of $28,000 today, or $3,300 each year for the next 15 years to reach that goal.

SOURCE: EDWARD D. JONES & CO.

Weekly Grocery Bills

Between January 1990 and January 1991, an American family's average weekly grocery bill was $79, up from $74 in 1986.

SOURCE: FOOD MARKETING INSTITUTE.

CEO's Paycheck—Proportionately Too High in United States

In Japan, the compensation of major CEOs is 17 times that of the average worker; in France and Germany, 23 to 25 times; in Britain, 35 times. In the United States, it's between 85 and 100-plus times!

SOURCE: WASHINGTON POST WRITERS GROUP, SEPTEMBER 3, 1991.

Save Something for the Flight Attendants

In 1990, United Airlines' CEO received $18.3 million in salary, bonuses, and a stock-based incentive plan, during a year in which the airline's profits fell 71 percent. His total earnings were 1,200 times what a new flight attendant was paid.

SOURCE: IBID.

Daily Rentals

Here are some average daily rental costs for various items. Prices vary, depending on region and store location.

Rent for Home	Price Range
Airless paint sprayer	$ 50–60
Carpet cleaner with upholstery tools	20–35
Floor sander	25–45
Floor polisher	10–30

Rent for Lawn	Price Range
Mulcher	70–120
Garden tiller	15–50
Tree sprayer	50–70

Rent for Party	
Portable bar	20–50
Chairs (depending on type)	1–5 each
Tables (depending on type)	5–15 each
Coffee maker	10–15
Silver punch bowl	30–50
Stork (for baby shower)	5–25
Tents and canopies (depending on size)	100–2,000

SOURCE: AMERICAN RENTAL ASSOCIATION.

The High Cost of 30 Seconds

The highest average cost of a 30-second ad on regularly scheduled network TV program in 1991 was as follows:

"Cheers"	$260,000
"NFL Monday Night Football"	255,000
"Roseanne	200,000
"60 Minutes"	200,000
"The Simpsons"	200,000
"Coach"	195,000

SOURCE; *ADVERTISING AGE.*

How Much Is a $20 Million Lottery Really Worth?

In a 1991 Ohio Super Lotto with a $20 million jackpot, it was determined that the odds of winning were 10.7 million to 1. This looks like a good bet—almost a 2 to 1 payoff on your money. But it's not as good as it appears because the $20 million payoff is made in 26 annual payments. To make these payments, the Ohio lottery sets aside $8,980,597, and with principal payments and compound interest on the unpaid portion, a total of $20 million is paid over the next 26 years.

SOURCE: AUTHORS' CALCULATIONS.

Minutes of Work for a Big Mac Around the World

The following is the amount of minutes a person must work in order to earn the money to buy a Big Mac:

City	Minutes	City	Minutes
Amsterdam	31	Milan	33
Bogotá	98	Nairobi	82
Bombay	131	New York	26
Cairo	103	Panama	66
Chicago	18	Paris	39
Frankfurt	22	São Paulo	106
Geneva	21	Seoul	30
Hong Kong	24	Singapore	70
Lagos	130	Tel Aviv	33
London	36	Tokyo	21
Los Angeles	20	Toronto	20
Madrid	54	Zurich	20
Mexico City	23		

SOURCE: *PRICES AND EARNINGS AROUND THE GLOBE*, UNION BANK OF SWITZERLAND, ZURICH, ECONOMIC RESEARCH DEPARTMENT, 1991.

Another Decade Older and Deeper in Debt

By the end of 1992, it was estimated that the United States' total debt outstanding, which includes government, business, and consumers, will reach $10.6 trillion, up from $3.9 trillion in 1980. Since 1980, when the outstanding debt was $17,116 per person, it rose to $42,277 by the end of 1991.

SOURCE: TAX FOUNDATION.

Not Too Thrifty Americans

In 1990, the average per capita savings in the United States was $4,201. This compares with $45,118 in Japan, the nation with the highest per capita savings in the world. Swiss citizens were a distant second with an average savings of $19,971. Other countries in the top ten in descending order were Denmark, France, Germany (only western part), Austria, Norway, Belgium, Singapore, and the Netherlands. In Western Europe, only Italy and Portugal were behind the United States. Canadians averaged $5,531 in U.S. dollars.

SOURCE: INTERNATIONAL SAVINGS BANK INSTITUTE.

Planning Ahead for Retirement

Let's say, for example, you think you need a $300,000 retirement fund for when you reach age 60. Let's also assume that you can earn an 8% rate of return each year. If you start to save at age 40, it will mean putting away $6,600 a year for the next 20 years. However, if you wait until age 55, it's going to take $51,150 for the next 5 years to accumulate the same amount.

SOURCE: AUTHORS' CALCULATIONS.

Deduct Interest Payments and Save Taxes

By allowing a deduction on interest of car payments, the borrower would save big bucks. The following is based on a 5-year, $12,000 at 9.75 percent interest, with a monthly payment of $253.49:

			Tax Savings		
Year	**Principal Paid**	**Interest Paid**	**15%**	**28%**	**31%**
1	$1,957.43	$1,084.05	$162.61	$303.53	$336.06
2	2,157.49	884.39	132.66	247.63	274.16
3	2,377.52	664.36	99.65	186.02	205.95
4	2,619.94	421.94	63.29	118.14	130.80
5	2,887.14	154.74	23.21	43.33	47.97
Totals	$12,000.00*	$3,209.48	$481.42	$898.65	$994.94

*Figure rounded

SOURCE: "HOW INTEREST DEDUCTION WOULD SAVE MONEY," *COLUMBUS DISPATCH*, DECEMBER 17, 1991.

11. Sporting Times

300 Strikeouts in Each of 3 Seasons

The first major league baseball pitcher to strike out 300 batters in 3 consecutive seasons was Sanford ("Sandy") Koufax of the Los Angeles Dodgers, who fanned 306 batters in 1963, 382 in 1965, and 307 in 1966.

SOURCE: JOSEPH NATHAN KANE. *FAMOUS FIRST FACTS*. WORLD BOOK, 1989.

First All-Star Major League Baseball Game

The first all-star major league baseball game was played on July 6, 1933, at Comiskey Park, Chicago. The American League defeated the National League 4–2. SOURCE: IBID.

First Major League Night Game

The first major league night game was played at Crosley Field, Cincinnati, Ohio, on May 24, 1935, between the Cincinnati Reds and the Philadelphia Phillies. SOURCE: IBID.

First Game in Which Majority of One Team Was Black

The first major league baseball game in which the majority of one team was black was played on July 17, 1954, between the

National League Brooklyn Dodgers and the Milwaukee Braves at Milwaukee, Wisconsin. The blacks played for the Dodgers. The Braves won by a score of 6–1. SOURCE: IBID.

First to Score More Than 4,000 Hits

The first baseball player to score more than 4,000 hits was Ty Cobb, who played in 3,033 games in 24 years, scoring 4,191 hits in his 11,429 times at bat. SOURCE: IBID.

First to Steal 100 Bases in a Season

The first baseball player to steal more than 100 bases in a season was Maurice ("Maury") Wills, shortstop for the National League Los Angeles Dodgers. Wills stole his 104th base on August 3, 1962. SOURCE: IBID.

2 Successive No-Hit, No-Run Games

John Samuel ("Johnny") Vander Meer, "the Dutch Master" of the National League Cincinnati Reds, on June 11, 1938, shut out Boston by a 3–0 in Cincinnati, Ohio, without giving up a hit. Only 3 men reached first base, all on walks. On June 15, 1938, he defeated the Brooklyn Dodgers in New York City, 6–0. SOURCE: IBID.

First Baseball Team

The first baseball team was the Knickerbocker Club of New York, organized on September 23, 1845. SOURCE: IBID.

No-Hit, No-Run, No-Walk, World Series Game

The first and only baseball player to pitch a perfect no-hit, no-run, no-walk World Series game was Donald James ("Don")

Larsen of the American League New York Yankees on October 8, 1956.

SOURCE: IBID.

3 World Series in a Row

The New York Yankees were the first team to win the World Series 3 times in a row: 1936, 1937, and 1938. Then they won 5 World Series in a row, from 1949 to 1953.

SOURCE: IBID.

All 9 Positions in 1 Game

The first baseball player to play all 9 positions in 1 game was Blanco Dagoberto ("Bert") Campaneris of the American League Kansas City Athletics, who played all positions in a 13-inning night game at Kansas City, Missouri, on September 8, 1965.

SOURCE: IBID.

Waiting for a Winning Season

The following list shows the number of years it took these expansion teams to have a winning season:

Kansas City Royals	3 years
Toronto Blue Jays	7 years
New York Mets	8 years
Seattle Pilots/Milwaukee Brewers	10 years
San Diego Padres	10 years
Montreal Expos	11 years
Houston Colt 45s/Astros	11 years

SOURCE: *USA TODAY* RESEARCH.

First Televised Baseball Game

New York's W2XBS televised the first major league baseball game between the Cincinnati Reds and the Brooklyn Dodgers on August 6, 1936.

SOURCE: JOSEPH NATHAN KANE. *FAMOUS FIRST FACTS*. WORLD BOOK, 1989.

Youngest/Oldest Baseball Players

The youngest major league player of all time was the Cincinnati pitcher Joe Nuxhall, who started his career in June 1944, at age 15.

The oldest player was Leroy ("Satchel") Paige, who pitched 3 scoreless innings for the Kansas City Athletics at the approximate age of 59. SOURCE: *GUINNESS BOOK OF WORLD RECORDS*, 1991.

First World Series

The World Series was officially staged in 1905 and continued annually between the winners of the National League and the American League. SOURCE: IBID.

Longest Baseball Game

The Chicago White Sox and the Milwaukee Brewers played a game that ran for 8 hours and 6 minutes on May 9, 1984. The White Sox won 7–6. SOURCE: BARBARA BERLINER, MELINDA COREY, AND GEORGE OCHOA. *THE BOOK OF ANSWERS.* PRENTICE HALL PRESS, 1990.

Jewish Player in the Majors

The first Jewish player in the major leagues was Lipman Pike in 1876. SOURCE: ANDREW POSTMAN AND LARRY STONE. *THE ULTIMATE BOOK OF SPORTS LISTS.* BANTAM BOOKS, 1990.

First Curveball

The first pitcher to throw a curveball was Candy Cummings in 1867. SOURCE: IBID.

Little Leaguer to Play in the Majors

In 1961, Joey Jay became the first Little League player to play in the major leagues. SOURCE: IBID.

"Play Ball!"

William Howard Taft was the first president to throw out the first ball of the season on April 14, 1910, in Washington, in a game against Philadelphia. SOURCE: IBID.

The Yankees' First World Series

The New York Yankees won their first World Series in 1923, and they continued to win 22 more times until 1978.

SOURCE: IBID.

Designated Hitter

On April 6, 1973, Ron Blomberg was the first designated hitter. He played for the New York Yankees. SOURCE IBID.

First Player to Die on the Diamond

Raymond Johnson Chapman, shortstop for the American League Cleveland Indians, was the first baseball player killed in a game. He was accidentally hit in the left side of his head by pitcher Carl William Mays of the American League New York Yankees in a game at the Polo Grounds, New York City, on August 16, 1920.

SOURCE: JOSEPH NATHAN KANE. *FAMOUS FIRST FACTS*. WORLD BOOK, 1989.

Longest Hitting Streak in Baseball

Joe DiMaggio of the American League New York Yankees holds the record for the longest hitting streak in baseball. His 56-consecutive-game streak began on May 15, 1941, and ended on July 16, 1941. He batted 223 times, scoring 15 home runs, had 4 three-baggers, 16 two-base hits, and 91 one-base hits. During this streak, he batted in 55 runs and his average was .408. Baseball experts consider it to be the record that is the most difficult to break. SOURCE: IBID.

Big Bucks for Roger Clemens

Roger Clemens starts 35 games a year and pitches 250 innings, tossing about 120 pitches each game. The Boston Red Sox pitcher's 1991 annual salary of $5.4 million breaks down to approximately $1,286 a pitch.

SOURCE: BILL SAPORITO, "THE OWNERS' NEW GAME IS MANAGING," *FORTUNE*, JULY 1, 1991.

First Army-Navy Football Game

The first Army-Navy football game was played November 29, 1890, at West Point, New York. Navy won 24–0.

SOURCE: JOSEPH NATHAN KANE. *FAMOUS FIRST FACTS*, WORLD BOOK, 1989.

Reliable Instant Replays

The first football game in which referees were permitted to use instant replays was the Hall of Fame Philadelphia Eagles game, July 29, 1978, at Canton, Ohio, when the Eagles defeated the National Football League Miami Dolphins 17–3.

SOUCE: IBID.

First All-Star Football Game

The first all-star football game was played on August 31, 1934, at Soldier Field, Chicago. The Chicago Bears played the College All-Stars to a 0–0 tie.

SOURCE: IBID.

Pro Football Hang Time for Punts

A good hang time (the time that the football is in the air) from the time it leaves the kicker's foot is 4.8 seconds.

SOURCE: ROBERT PALCIC, SPECIAL TEAMS COACH, OHIO STATE UNIVERSITY FOOTBALL TEAM.

Hang Time for Kickoffs

In both professional football and major college football, if the ball is in the air from the time it is kicked on the 35-yard line until it reaches the opposing team's goal line, a period of 4.2 seconds is considered good hang time. SOURCE: IBID.

Football Snap Times for Punting

In both professional and college football, the snap time (the time in which the football leaves the center's hands and is caught by the punter) is .8 seconds. The distance between the punter and center is approximately 15 yards. It takes another 1.2 seconds for the punter to catch and kick the football, which means a total of 2 seconds has lapsed. SOURCE: IBID.

Extra Points and Field Goal Times

The holder positions the ball approximately 7 yards behind the line of scrimmage. It takes .5 seconds from the snap until the holder catches the ball. Another .7 seconds expires before the kicker kicks the ball, for a total of 1.2 seconds.

SOURCE: IBID.

A $3.64 Billion Football Deal

In March 1990, the National Football League made a deal worth $3.64 billion for 4 years' coverage by the 5 major TV and cable networks, ABC, CBS, NBC, ESPN, TBS. This averaged out to $26.1 million for each league team in the first year, escalating to $39.1 million in the fourth.

SOURCE: *GUINNESS BOOK OF WORLD RECORDS*, 1991.

First Professional Football Game

The first professional football game was played on September 3, 1895, at Latrobe, Pennsylvania, between the Latrobe Young Men's Christian Association and the Jeannette (Pa.) Athletic Club. The former won 12–0. SOURCE: JOSEPH NATHAN KANE.

FAMOUS FIRST FACTS. WORLD BOOK, 1989.

98-Yard Punt

The first football player to punt 98 yards was Steve O'Neal, New York Jet rookie (NFL), who punted 98 yards against the Denver Broncos on September 21, 1969, at the Mile High Stadium, Denver, Colorado. Denver won 21–19. SOURCE: IBID.

Longest Winning Streak by a Major College Football Team

From 1953 to 1957, the University of Oklahoma won 47 straight games overall, both in and out of the Big Eight Conference, to set an all-time national collegiate record for consecutive victories.

SOURCE: ROBERT L. SHOOK AND RONALD L. BINGAMAN. *TOTAL COMMITMENT*. FREDERICK FELL PUBLISHERS, 1975.

First Super Bowl Touchdown

In 1967, Max McGee of the Green Bay Packers scored the first Super Bowl touchdown.

SOURCE: ANDREW POSTMAN AND LARRY STONE. *THE ULTIMATE BOOK OF SPORTS LISTS*. BANTAM BOOKS, 1990.

Longest Football Game

The longest football game was played on December 25, 1971, between the Miami Dolphins and the Kansas City Chiefs; the game lasted 82 minutes and 40 seconds. It went into a second period of sudden death before Garo Yepremian kicked a field goal and won the game for the Dolphins, 27–24

SOURCE: BARBARA BERLINER, MELINDA COREY, AND GEORGE OCHOA. *THE BOOK OF ANSWERS*. PRENTICE HALL PRESS, 1990.

Average Turnovers

From 1985 to 1989 NFL teams averaged about 36 turnovers each season. SOURCE: ELIAS SPORTS BUREAU.

Better to Score First

The 1989 record of NFL teams that scored first in a game: 116 wins, 65 losses, 1 tie. SOURCE: NFL, *USA TODAY* RESEARCH.

Instant Replay Not So Instant

The average delay per game in the NFL due to the instant replay was 1 minute and 55 seconds. SOURCE: NFL OFFICIALS.

Short Football Careers

The average career in football is just over 3 years.

SOURCE: NFL PLAYERS ASSOCIATION.

First Basketball Game to Be Televised

New York's W2XBS televised the first basketball game at Madison Square Garden between Fordham University and the University of Pittsburgh on February 28, 1940.

SOURCE: JOSEPH NATHAN KANE. *FAMOUS FIRST FACTS*. WORLD BOOK, 1989.

First Five-Man Game

The first intercollegiate basketball five-man team game was played on January 16, 1896, in Iowa City, Iowa. The University of Chicago defeated the University of Iowa by a score of 15–12.

SOURCE: IBID.

First NBA Black Player

The first NBA black player was Charles Henry Cooper, an all-star player who was drafted on April, 24, 1950, by the Boston

Celtics and who played his first game on November 1, 1950, in Fort Wayne, Indiana.

SOURCE: IBID.

3,000 in One Season, 4,000 in the Next

The first NBA basketball player to score more than 3,000 points in one season was Wilt Chamberlain of the Philadelphia Warriors. Wilt the Stilt scored 3,033 points in the 1960–1961 season. He was also the first player to score more than 4,000 points in one season! Chamberlain scored 4,029 points during the 1961–1962 season.

SOURCE: IBID.

Scoring 30 Points

Scoring 30 points or more by 1 player happened 671 times in the 1989–1990 NBA season.

SOURCE: NATIONAL BASKETBALL ASSOCIATION.

Disqualification

In the 1989–1990 NBA season 19 players were disqualified.

SOURCE: IBID.

First Woman Dunker

Georgeann Wells of West Virginia University was the first woman to dunk a basketball in official competition. She dunked in a game against the University of Charleston on December 21, 1983.

SOURCE: ANDREW POSTMAN AND LARRY STONE. *THE ULTIMATE BOOK OF SPORTS LISTS*. BANTAM BOOKS, 1990.

Highest Scoring Basketball Game

The highest scoring pro basketball game occurred in 1983, when the Detroit Pistons beat the Denver Nuggets, 186 to 183.

SOURCE: BARBARA BERLINER, MELINDA COREY, AND GEORGE OCHOA. *THE BOOK OF ANSWERS*. PRENTICE HALL PRESS, 1990.

Average NBA Career

On opening day of the 1989–1990 season, 351 players on the roster averaged 3.95 years of experience.

SOURCE: BILL KREIFELDT, CLIPPERS PR DIRECTOR.

Going Overtime

In the 1989–1990 NBA season there were 56 single-overtime games, 2 double-overtime games, 1 triple-overtime game, and 1 five-overtime game. 1,107 games are played in a season.

SOURCE: NATIONAL BASKETBALL ASSOCIATION.

The NBA Norm

The average NBA player in 1989 was 6 feet 9 inches tall, 215 pounds, 27 years old, and had been playing ball in the NBA for an average of 4 years.

SOURCE: IBID.

By a Point or Two

From 1981 to 1989, 5 NBA championship games were decided by 1 or 2 points.

SOURCE: *1990 SPORTS ALMANAC.*

NCAA Tournament Attendance

The average NCAA basketball tournament attendance in 1989 was 18,586 people.

SOURCE: NCAA.

Longest Boxing Match

The longest recorded fight with gloves occurred when Andy Bowen got into the ring with Jack Burke in New Orleans, April 6–7, 1893. The fight lasted 110 rounds, and went on for 7 hours, 19 minutes, from 9:15 P.M. to 4:34 A.M. The fight was declared no contest when the fighters were unable to continue.

SOURCE: *GUINNESS BOOK OF WORLD RECORDS*, 1990.

First Title Fight

The first world heavyweight title fight with 3-ounce gloves and 3-minute rounds was between John L. Sullivan and Dominick McCaffrey on August 29, 1885, in Cincinnati, Ohio. It went 6 rounds and Sullivan won.

SOURCE: *GUINNESS BOOK OF WORLD RECORDS*, 1991.

Shortest World Title Fights

The shortest world title fight was 45 seconds, when Lloyd Honeyghan beat Gene Hatcher in an IBF welterweight bout at Marbella, Spain, on August 30, 1987.

The shortest heavyweight world title fight was the James J. Jeffries-Hack Finnegan bout at Detroit, Michigan, on April 6, 1990, won by Jeffries in 55 seconds. SOURCE: IBID.

Fastest Boxing Bucks

The revenues of the world heavyweight fight to be split between Mike Tyson and Michael Spinks at Convention Hall, Atlantic City, New Jersey, on June 27, 1988 were estimated at approximately $35.8 million. $22 million went to Tyson and $13.8 million to Spinks, who was knocked out after 1 minute, 31 seconds of the first round. This averages about $151,000 a second for Spinks and about $241,000 a second for Tyson!

SOURCE: AUTHORS' CALCULATIONS.

Longest Reign

Joe Louis's heavyweight duration record of 11 years, 252 days stands for all divisions.

SOURCE: *GUINNESS BOOK OF WORLD RECORDS*, 1991.

Men Run Faster Nowadays

The winning time of the men's 5,000-meter race at the 1912 Olympics was 14 minutes, 36.6 seconds. The winner was Hannes

Kolehmainen of Finland. At the 1988 Olympics the time was 13 minutes, 11.7 seconds, by John Ngugi, Kenya.

SOURCE: *1991 INFORMATION PLEASE ALMANAC*. HOUGHTON MIFFLIN, 1991.

Was Achilles a Jogger?

A jogger's heel strikes the ground 1,500 times a mile, or 10,000 times an hour. During a 1-hour period, he or she contacts the ground with 4.5 million cumulative foot-pounds of force.

SOURCE: MIKE FEINSILBER AND WILLIAM B. MEAD. *AMERICAN AVERAGES*. DOUBLEDAY, 1980.

Getting Older—Getting Faster (Boys, That Is)

10-year-old females run the 50-yard dash in an average 8.9 seconds; 10-year-old males run it in 8.6 seconds; 17-year-old females run the 50-yard dash in an average 8.2 seconds; 17-year-old males run it in 6.7 seconds.

SOURCE: *YOUTH INDICATORS—1988: TRENDS IN THE WELL-BEING OF AMERICAN YOUTH*. OFFICE OF EDUCATIONAL RESEARCH AND IMPROVEMENT. U.S. DEPARTMENT OF EDUCATION.

Slow Children

50 percent of females and 30 percent of males ages 6 to 12 cannot run a mile in less than 10 minutes.

SOURCE: *USA TODAY*, MARCH 15, 1990.

Fastest Runners

A female has run 100 meters in 10.48 seconds. A male has run it in 9.92 seconds. A female has run a mile in 4 minutes, 15.71 seconds. A male has run it in 3 minutes, 46.32 seconds. A female has run a marathon in 2 hours, 21 minutes, 6 seconds; a male has run it in 2 hours, 6 minutes, 50 seconds.

SOURCE: *THE WORLD ALMANAC AND BOOK OF FACTS*, 1990.

Americans on the Run

In 1988, there were between 31.7 and 34.2 million runners in the United States. SOURCE: AMERICAN SPORTS DATA, INC.

Golfers Earn a Million

Jack Nicklaus was the first golfer to amass $1 million in career earnings in 1970, after taking second place in the Bing Crosby Pro-Am.

The first woman golfer to reach $1 million in career earnings was Kathy Whitworth, who took third place in the U.S. Women's Open in 1981.

SOURCE: ANDREW POSTMAN AND LARRY STONE. *THE ULTIMATE BOOK OF SPORTS LISTS*. BANTAM BOOKS, 1990.

Four Holes-in-One on the Same PGA Hole

On June 16, 1989, 4 holes-in-one were recorded in the U.S. Open in Rochester, New York's Oak Hill Country Club. The odds of 4 PGA Tour players doing it on the same hole on the same day are 1 in 332,000. SOURCE: *GOLF DIGEST*.

First 9 Holes Played by Jack Nicklaus

At age 10, champion golfer Jack Nicklaus carded a 51 in the first 9 holes he ever played. SOURCE: GOLDEN BEAR INTERNATIONAL.

Jack Nicklaus's First Professional Golf Tournament

In his first professional golf start in the Los Angeles Open on January 5–8, 1962, Nicklaus won $33.33. His total winnings for the year were $61,868 for third place plus $50,000 he picked up with a World Series of Golf victory. He was named Rookie of the Year for 1962. SOURCE: IBID.

Record Appearances on Cover of Golf Magazine

Jack Nicklaus appeared on the cover of *Golf* for a record total of 24 times between 1960 and 1988. His name was first mentioned in the magazine in the November 1959 issue in an article titled "The Bright Promise of College Golf" by Charles Maier.

SOURCE: "IN OUR WORDS," *GOLF*, SEPTEMBER 1988.

Most Tour Victories on Golf Circuit

Sam Snead has won the most PGA tournaments with 84 wins. In second place is Jack Nicklaus with 71 victories.

SOURCE: RICHARD V. LEVIN, "BEAR FACTS," *GOLF*, SEPTEMBER 1988.

Most Major Championships in Golf Career and Three "Grand Slams"

Jack Nicklaus has won 20 major championships, including 6 Masters, 5 PGA Championships, 4 U.S. Opens, 3 British Opens, and 2 U.S. Amateur championships. Bobby Jones ranks second with 13 major titles. Nicklaus is the only golfer to win 3 Grand Slams; no one else has done it more than once. SOURCE: IBID.

Winning at the Last Minute

The odds against a hockey team winning in the last 5 minutes are 20 to 1 and in the last 2 minutes are 40 to 1.

SOURCE: SPORTS PRODUCTS, INC., NORWALK, CONNECTICUT.

Penalty Shots

Of the 10,080 National Hockey League games played during the regular season for the 6-year period ending in 1989, 106 penalty shots were taken and only 45 were made. Based on these figures, the chances of making a penalty shot in the NHL are about 42 percent. SOURCE: NATIONAL HOCKEY LEAGUE.

Most Goals Scored

Gordon Howe of the Detroit Red Wings scored 801 goals in his 25-year career, from 1946 to 1971.

SOURCE: BARBARA BERLINER, MELINDA COREY, AND GEORGE OCHOA. *THE BOOK OF ANSWERS*. PRENTICE HALL PRESS, 1990.

More Than 100 Points in a Season

The first hockey player to score more than 100 points in a season was Gordon Howe of the National Hockey League Detroit Red Wings, who scored 103 points in the 1968–1969 season.

SOURCE: JOSEPH NATHAN KANE. *FAMOUS FIRST FACTS*. WORLD BOOK, 1989.

6 Goals in 1 Game

The first hockey player to score 6 goals in 1 game was Syd Howe of the National Hockey League Detroit Red Wings, who scored 6 goals on February 3, 1944 in a game with the New York Rangers at Olympia Stadium, Detroit, Michigan. The score was Red Wings 12, Rangers 2.

SOURCE: IBID.

First Black Player in Organized Hockey

The first black player in organized hockey was Arthur Dorrington, who signed with the Atlantic City Seagulls of the Eastern Amateur League on November 15, 1950, Atlantic City, New Jersey; he played for them in 1950 and 1951.

SOURCE: IBID.

Average Winning Ticket on a Horse Race

In 1989, the average amount of money paid on a winning ticket was $8.80.

SOURCE: THOROUGHBRED RACING ASSOCIATION.

America's Skiers

In 1989, there were 21 million skiers in the United States.

SOURCE: NATIONAL SPORTING GOODS ASSOCIATION SPORTS PARTICIPATION STUDY.

Closest Finish

The closest finish in the Indianapolis 500 was in the 1982 race when the winner, Gordon Johncock, crossed the finish line just .16 seconds before runner-up Rick Mears.

SOURCE: *GUINNESS BOOK OF WORLD RECORDS*, 1990.

The Average High-School Coach

The average high-school coach is a 36-year-old white male with 12 years' coaching experience. Almost 70 percent of them participated in varsity athletics in college and about 97 percent in high school.

SOURCE: *USA TODAY*.

Mush

The famous annual Iditarod Trail Sled Dog Race begins in Anchorage and ends 1,163 miles later in Nome. In 1991, Rick Swenson, who finished first among 75 mushers, was clocked in at a time of 12 days, 16 hours, and 34 minutes. That's an average of 91 miles per day; on a 12-hour day that comes to about 7.5 mph. It was a record 5 wins for Swenson in the famed event that re-creates a historic 1925 relay carrying lifesaving serum by dogsled during a diphtheria epidemic. During the race, there was a wind-chill temperature of 50 degrees below zero.

SOURCE: ASSOCIATED PRESS.

A Long 30 Seconds

The average sports parachutist often free-falls for 30 seconds, routinely starting from 7,200 feet in the air. During that time, he or she drops at a speed of 120 mph or even 200 mph in a dive, before pulling the rip cord at 2,500 feet. The average chutist takes 6 to 10 jumps per outing.

SOURCE: MIKE FEINSILBER AND WILLIAM B. MEAD. *AMERICAN AVERAGES*. DOUBLEDAY, 1980.

Fastest Pit Stop

Bobby Unser took 4 seconds to take on fuel on lap 10 of the Indianapolis 500 on May 30, 1976.

SOURCE: *GUINNESS BOOK OF WORLD RECORDS*, 1990.

Betting on Sports

During 1985, 24 percent of women and 36 percent of men bet on sports events.

SOURCE: *SPORTS ILLUSTRATED SPORTS POLL '86*. LIEBERMAN RESEARCH.

Fastest Swimmers

A female has swum 100 meters in 54.73 seconds; a male has swum the distance in 48.42 seconds. A female has swum the 200-meter butterfly in 57.93 seconds; a male has done it in 52.84 seconds. A female has swum the 100-meter backstroke in 1 minute, .59 seconds; a male has swum it in 54.91 seconds.

SOURCE: *THE WORLD ALMANAC AND BOOK OF FACTS*, 1990.

Pool Sharks

An estimated 10 million different people play pool each year.

SOURCE: *BILLIARDS DIGEST*.

Cross-Country Skiers

Less than 4 percent of the population cross-country skis, and they average only 7.2 days each year.

SOURCE: AMERICAN SPORTS DATA.

Alpine Skiers

About 7 percent of the population skis downhill. They ski an average of about 7 days a season. SOURCE: IBID.

Biggest Endorsement Deal in Sports

Michael Jordan received more than $3 million from Nike, the most any athlete was paid in a single deal.

SOURCE: PETER NEWCOMB. "MADONNA IS THE MODEL," *FORBES*, AUGUST 19, 1991, P. 18.

Oldest Player to Win a PGA Tournament

In 1965, Sam Snead became the oldest player ever to win a regular PGA event. He was 53 years old when he won the Greensboro Open. In 1974, at age 62, he finished third in the PGA championship, just 2 strokes behind winner Lee Trevino.

SOURCE: ROBERT L. SHOOK AND RONALD BINGAMAN. *TOTAL COMMITMENT*. FREDERICK FELL PUBLISHERS, 1975.

Golf Earnings Then and Now

Sam Snead was the PGA's leading money winner in 1949 when his earnings totaled $31,593. He repeated as the PGA's top money winner in 1950 when his earnings were $35,758. In comparison, in the PGA Western Open that ended on July 7, 1991, the top 10 money winners and their earnings from the tournament were Russ Cochran ($180,000), Greg Norman ($108,000), Fred Couples ($68,000), Bob Gilder ($48,000), D. A. Webring ($32,750), John Huston ($32,750), Kenny Knox ($32,750), Nick Price ($32,750), Dave Barr ($32,750), and Gary Halberg ($32,750).

That same day, in the Kroger Senior Classic, the top 5 winners and their earnings were Al Geiberger ($90,000), Larry Laoretti ($51,200), Milt Barber ($35,083), Harold Henning ($35,083), and Dale Douglass ($35,083).

In the Celebrity Championship that ended on July 7, 1991,

the top 2 money winners were Rick Rhoden ($75,000) and Bill Lambeer ($36,000). In the LPGA Jamie Farr Toledo Classic, the top 2 winners were Alice Miller ($52,500) and Deb Richard ($32,375). A total of 19 golfers won more in a single tournament in the week ending July 7, 1991, than Sam Snead won in 1949 when he was the PGA's leading money winner!

SOURCES: AUTHORS' CALCULATIONS AND *USA TODAY*, JULY 8, 1991.

World's Highest-Paid Athletes in 1991

Athlete	1991 Total Income (in millions)	Sport
Evander Holyfield	$60.5	Boxing
Mike Tyson	31.5	Boxing
Michael Jordan	16.	Basketball
George Foreman	14.5	Boxing
Ayrton Senna	13.	Auto racing
Alain Prost	11.	Auto racing
Razor Ruddock	10.2	Boxing
Arnold Palmer	9.3	Golf
Nigel Mansell	9.	Auto racing
Jack Nicklaus	8.5	Golf

SOURCE: PETER NEWCOMB, "MADONNA IS THE MODEL," *FORBES*, AUGUST 19, 1991.

Highest-Paid Athletes for Endorsement in 1991

Rank	Athlete	Sport	Earnings
1	Michael Jordan	Basketball	$13.2 million
2	Arnold Palmer	Golf	9.0 million
3	Jack Nicklaus	Golf	8.0 million
4	Greg Norman	Golf	7.0 million
5	Andre Agassi	Tennis	6.5 million

SOURCE: IBID.

Calories Used Per Minute According to Body Weight

Weight in Pounds

Activity	**100**	**120**	**150**	**170**	**200**	**220**
Volleyball (moderate)	2.3	2.7	3.4	3.9	4.6	5.0
Walking (3 mph)	2.7	3.2	4.0	4.6	5.4	5.9
Table tennis	2.7	3.2	4.0	4.6	5.4	5.9
Bicycling (5.5 mph)	3.1	3.8	4.7	5.3	6.3	6.9
Calisthenics	3.3	3.9	4.9	5.6	6.6	7.2
Skating (moderate)	3.6	4.3	5.4	6.1	7.2	7.9
Golf	3.6	4.3	5.4	6.1	7.2	7.9
Walking (4 mph)	3.9	4.6	5.8	6.6	7.8	8.5
Tennis	4.5	5.4	6.8	7.7	9.1	10.0
Canoeing (4 mph)	4.6	5.6	7.0	7.9	9.3	10.2
Swimming (breaststroke)	4.6	5.7	7.2	8.1	9.6	10.5
Bicycling (10 mph)	5.4	6.5	8.1	9.2	10.8	11.9
Swimming (crawl)	5.8	6.9	8.7	9.8	11.6	12.7
Jogging (11-min. mile)	6.1	7.3	9.1	10.4	12.2	13.4
Handball	6.3	7.6	9.5	10.7	12.7	13.9
Racquetball	6.3	7.6	9.5	10.7	12.7	13.9
Skiing (downhill)	6.3	7.6	9.5	10.7	12.7	13.9
Mountain climbing	6.6	8.0	10.0	11.3	13.3	14.6
Squash	6.8	8.1	10.2	11.5	13.6	14.9
Skiing (cross-country)	7.2	8.7	10.8	12.3	14.5	15.9
Running (8-min. mile)	9.4	11.3	14.1	16.0	18.8	20.7

Note: Many other factors, including air temperature, clothing, and the vigor with which a person exercises, can cause an increase or decrease in the number of calories used. SOURCE: *THE WORLD ALMANAC AND BOOK OF FACTS*, 1991.

America's Most Participated-in Sport

In 1990, 42.6 million Americans participated in exercise walking, now the most popular sport in the country.

SOURCE: NATIONAL SPORTING GOODS ASSOCIATION.

Progression of the Men's 100-Meter World Record

Time	Runner	Country	Date
10.6 seconds	Donald Lippincott	United States	July 6, 1912
10.4	Charles Paddock	United States	April 23, 1921
10.3	Percy Williams	Canada	August 9, 1930
10.2	Jesse Owens	United States	June 20, 1936
10.1	Willie Williams	United States	August 3, 1956
10.0	Armin Hary	West Germany	June 21, 1960
9.9	Jim Hines	United States	June 20, 1968
9.95	Jim Hines	United States	October 14, 1968
9.93	Calvin Smith	United States	July 3, 1983
9.92	Carl Lewis	United States	September 24, 1988
9.90	Leroy Burrell	United States	June 14, 1991
9.86	Carl Lewis	United States	August 25, 1991

SOURCE: INTERNATIONAL AMATEUR ATHLETIC FEDERATION.

Baseball—America's Favorite Pastime

From 1988 to 1990, there was a 33.3 percent increase in the number of baseball participants between the ages of 18 and 34. For the 6- to 11-year-olds, there was a 4.6 percent increase. To be included in the survey, a participant had to play the game 52 days or more per year. In 1990, 1.3 million 6- to 11-year-olds did so, whereas 600,000 in the 18- to 34-year group did.

SOURCE: SPORTING GOODS MANUFACTURERS ASSOCIATION.

Days Spent on the Links

22.2 million Americans play golf a total of 393.7 million days, averaging 17.7 days a year. 6.8 million golfers are considered "heavy" golfers, playing more than 20 times a year.

SOURCE: STUDY BY PROFESSOR ROD WARNICK, UNIVERSITY OF MASSACHUSETTS.

Professional Football Is a Young Man's Sport

The 1990 percentage of players based on number of years experience in the NFL is:

Year	Percent
Rookie	17%
2nd	14%
3rd	13%
4th	13%
5th	10%
6th	9%
7th	7%
8th	6%
9th	4%
10th	3%
10th plus	5%

SOURCE: NFL PLAYERS ASSOCIATION.

Highest Scoring Basketball Game

The Troy State Trojans (Troy, Alabama) scored a 258–141 victory over DeVry Institute on January 12, 1992, marking the first basketball game in history that an NCAA team ever passed the 200-point mark. The Division II team lead at the halftime by a 123–53 margin and did even better in the second half with 135 points. The game total points was 399, a hair under 10 points a minute. A total of 223 points were registered during the second half, averaging more than 11 points a minute. That's more than 1 point every 6 seconds! SOURCE: ASSOCIATED PRESS.

Old Pro Golfers Never Quit . . .

In 1991, the six oldest professional golfers of the Senior PGA Tour were: Sam Snead, 79; Jerry Barber, 75; Julius Boros, 71; Charlie Sifford, 69; Doug Ford, 69; and Mike Fetchick, 69.

SOURCE: *USA TODAY* RESEARCH.

12. Odds and Ends

Eating Habits

The average American consumed 72.2 pounds of beef in 1980; in 1989 the amount dropped nearly 10 percent to 65.1 pounds. In comparison, per capita consumption of chicken is 47.5 pounds, up from 34.9 in 1980; fish consumption is also up at 15 pounds compared with 12.8 pounds in 1980.

SOURCE: KARIN A. WELZEL, "BOMBARDED BEEF BOUNCES BACK," *COLUMBUS DISPATCH*, MAY 15, 1991.

Tossed Out Third-Class Mail

In 1990, Americans received 63 billion pieces of third-class mail and tossed out an estimated 15 percent of it unopened, destroying an estimated 5 million trees and taking up about a million cubic yards of landfill, more than the capacity of the world's largest supertanker. SOURCE: U.S. POSTAL SERVICE.

The Typical Survey

In the United States a nationwide survey is normally completed in a period of about 10 days.

SOURCE: *A GUIDE TO PUBLIC OPINION POLLS*—GALLUP.

Tons of Flakes

In Disney World, more than 9 tons of artificial snow fall daily at Sea World's Penguin Encounter. SOUCE: *TIME*, MAY 27, 1991.

Limited Immigration

Immigration to the United States is numerically limited to 270,000 persons per year. Within this quota there is an annual limitation of 20,000 for each country.

SOURCE: *THE WORLD ALMANAC AND BOOK OF FACTS*, 1991.

How Much Water Is Used?

The average residence uses 107,000 gallons of water each year. The average person uses 168 gallons of water daily.

It takes 5 to 7 gallons to flush a toilet.

It takes 25 to 50 gallons to take a shower.

It takes 2 gallons to brush the teeth if the water is kept running.

It takes 20 gallons to wash dishes by hand, whereas it takes 10 gallons to run a dishwasher.

SOURCE: AMERICAN WATER WORKS ASSOCIATION.

New Business

During the 1980s, an average of 620,000 new businesses opened up each year. SOURCE: SMALL BUSINESS ADMINISTRATION.

Longest Term in Office

Franklin Delano Roosevelt served as president of the United States for 12 years, 39 days, from 1933 to his death in 1945.

SOURCE: *GUINNESS BOOK OF WORLD RECORDS*, 1991.

One Step at a Time

Each of the average person's feet hits the floor 7,000 times a day. SOURCE: MIKE FEINSILBER AND WILLIAM B. MEAD. *AMERICAN AVERAGES*. DOUBLEDAY, 1980.

Want to Live to 100?

49 percent of Americans say they want to live to be 100 years old. SOURCE: MEDIA GENERAL AND ASSOCIATED PRESS POLL.

Lots of Mail

The average person receives an average of 598 pieces of mail each year. SOURCE: U.S. POSTAL SERVICE.

Dead Letter Mail

75,100,000 pieces of mail end up in the dead-letter office each year. SOURCE: U.S. POSTAL SERVICE.

Toys from Cracker Jack

Cracker Jack has given away 16 billion toys in its boxes since 1912. SOURCE: BORDEN, INC.

Millions of "Yesterdays"

The Beatles' "Yesterday" has been broadcast 4,600,000 times since 1970. SOURCE: BROADCAST MUSIC, INC.

Celebrating Elvis's Birthday

Every year 60 wreaths are delivered to Graceland on Elvis's birthday. SOURCE: GRACELAND.

Lotsa 'Za

Each day 75 acres of pizza are consumed in the United States. SOURCE: TIM PARKER. *IN ONE DAY.* HOUGHTON MIFFLIN, 1984.

Hello, Officer

10 percent of female and 20 percent of male drivers receive a traffic ticket each year.

SOURCE: TOM AND NANCY BIRACREE. *ALMANAC OF THE AMERICAN PEOPLE*. FACTS ON FILE, 1988.

Sweet Habit

50 percent of females and 62 percent of males eat candy at least once a week.

SOURCE: *NEWS FROM THE NATIONAL CONFECTIONERS ASSOCIATION.*

Gone to the Grocery Store

90 percent of females and 69 percent of males go food shopping weekly. SOURCE: *ROPER REPORTS*, DECEMBER 1989.

Getting Flowers

Females visit florists an average of 2.8 times a year, whereas males do so an average of 3.8 times a year.

SOURCE: *SOCIETY OF AMERICAN FLORISTS FLORAL MARKETING REPORT*. 1985.

Shortest Term in Office

William Henry Harrison was in office for only 32 days, from March 4 to April 4, 1841.

SOURCE: *GUINNESS BOOK OF WORLD RECORDS*, 1991.

Youngest President to Assume Office

The youngest president to assume office was Theodore Roosevelt, who was only 42 years, 236 days old when he became president. He held office from 1901 to 1909. SOURCE: IBID.

Oldest Elected President

Ronald Wilson Reagan was the oldest president to be elected. He was 69 years, 349 days old and served from 1981 to 1989.

SOURCE: IBID.

Sex Ed

Secondary schools provide students an average of 6.5 hours a year on sex education, and fewer than 2 of those hours focus on contraception and the prevention of sexually transmitted disease.

SOURCE: ALAN GUTTMACHER INSTITUTE, NEW YORK.

Snap Happy

In 1988, Americans took more than 15 billion photos, which is about 63 pictures per person.

SOURCE: *U.S. NEWS & WORLD REPORT*, NOVEMBER 27, 1989.

Serving on Jury Duty

In 1988, 7 percent of Americans were called for jury duty, and 2 percent of females and 3 percent of males have served.

SOURCE: *ROPER REPORTS*, FEBRUARY 1989.

Increase in Endangered Species

The number of endangered species in previous years:

1970–123
1975–139
1980–224
1985–267
1990–355

SOURCE: U.S. FISH AND WILDLIFE SERVICE.

What Is a Billion?

1 billion seconds equals about 31.7 years!
1 billion days equals more than 2.7 million years!
1 billion mph is 1.5 times the speed of light!

SOURCE: *CHICAGO TRIBUNE*, NEWS REPORTS.

Raising the Temp

If current rates of fossil-fuel burning and rain forest destruction continue, the carbon dioxide concentration in the air could increase 50 percent by the year 2050, enough to raise the global temperature by an average of 4 to 9 degrees.

SOURCE: ENVIRONMENTAL PROTECTION AGENCY.

Recycle It

Every year each American throws away 1,200 pounds of garbage; only 10 percent of it is recycled. SOURCE: IBID.

Polluting the Air

Every year American businesses release 2.4 billion pounds of pollutants into the air, or about 10 pounds for every man, woman, and child. SOURCE: IBID.

Fastest Publishing

The fastest time in which a hardcover book has been published is 43 hours, 15 minutes in the case of *The ITN Book of the Royal Wedding*, published by Michael O'Mara. Typesetting began at 2:00 P.M. on July 24, 1986, and the books were on sale at 9:15 A.M. 2 days later.

SOURCE: *GUINNESS BOOK OF WORLD RECORDS*, 1990.

Slowest Publishing

The slowest-published book was the German dictionary *Deutsche Wortherbuch*, begun by the Brothers Grimm in 1854 and finished in 1971. SOURCE: IBID.

Not a Good Place to Build

Due to the ground shifting, the Leaning Tower of Pisa, built in 1174, started to tilt almost immediately after its completion. The tower is tilted about 13 feet from the perpendicular, and annually has tilted about 1.19 mm. or .047 inches since measurements began in 1918. Experts say the tower will not topple for more than a century. SOURCE: *COLUMBUS DISPATCH*, MARCH 31, 1991.

The Average-Aged Home

The median age for all homes is 25 years. Blacks tend to live in slightly older homes—about 31 years old.

SOURCE: 1987 CENSUS BUREAU SURVEY.

America Loses an Hour

On March 31, 1918, America lost an hour when it suddenly became 3:00 A.M. Clocks across the continent were set forward 1 hour in a government move to "save daylight." In 1966 the U.S. Congress declared that daylight saving time would begin on the last Sunday in April and that clocks would return to standard time on the following "last Sunday in October."

SOURCE: DAVID WALLECHINSKY AND IRVING WALLACE. *THE PEOPLE'S ALMANAC #3*, BANTAM BOOKS, 1981.

The 8-Foot, 11-Inch Giant

At birth, on February 22, 1918, Robert Wadlow was a normal 8½-pound baby. Things changed quickly, however. At 6 months he weighed 30 pounds; at 1 year, 44 pounds; at 18 months, 62 pounds. His first thorough examination came at age 5, when he stood 5 feet, 4 inches tall and weighed 105 pounds. He reached 6 feet at age 8, and at 10 he was 6 feet, 5 inches tall, weighing 210 pounds. At age 12 he was diagnosed as having excessive pituitary gland secretion, and he continued to grow about 3 inches a year until he died. He passed 7 feet before turning 13, and at 16 he was 7 feet, 10½ inches, the tallest person in the United States. At 19 he became the tallest person ever measured, 8 feet, 5½ inches. Several weeks before Wadlow died, he reached 8 feet, 11 inches, weighing 439 pounds. He died in Michigan on July 15, 1940. SOURCE: *GUINNESS BOOK OF WORLD RECORDS*, 1990.

Longest Lease

The longest lease on record is 10 million years for a plot for a sewage tank adjoining Columb Barracks, Ireland, signed on December 3, 1888. SOURCE: IBID.

What a Crowd

Luciano Pavarotti set a world record with 165 curtain calls after singing at the West Berlin Opera in Germany on February 24, 1988. The audience of 2,000 stood and cheered for 67 minutes. SOURCE: *GUINNESS BOOK OF WORLD RECORDS*, 1991.

Longest Running Musical

The longest running musical is the off-Broadway show, *The Fantasticks* by Tom Jones and Harvey Schmidt, which held its 10,864th performance on June 8, 1986, after 26 years. The show was scheduled to close that day, but the announcement stirred up so much demand for tickets that the musical had to stay open indefinitely. It set a record by playing 12,075 performances on May 3, 1989, when it started its thirtieth year in the same theater, the Sullivan Street Playhouse in Greenwich Village, New York City. SOURCE: *GUINNESS BOOK OF WORLD RECORDS*, 1990.

Longest Running Film

The longest continuing running film at 1 cinema is *Emmanuelle,* which opened on June 26, 1974, at the Paramount City, Paris, and closed on February 26, 1985. SOURCE: IBID.

Fastest Camera

A camera built for research into high-power lasers by the Blackett Laboratory of Imperial College of Science and Technology, London, registers images at the rate of 33 million per second. SOURCE: IBID.

Service Performance

In 1988, the U.S. Postal Service's on-time performance was 95 percent for local overnight delivery, 86 percent for 2-day delivery within 600 miles, and 89 percent on time for cross-country delivery within 3 days. SOURCE: The U.S. POSTAL SERVICE.

Mailmen Get Exercise

The average letter carrier walks an average of 5.2 miles per day on delivery. SOURCE: NATIONAL ASSOCIATION OF LETTER CARRIERS.

Average Length of Retirement

The average length of retirement for a man at age 62 is 17 years and 20 years for a woman.

SOURCE: SHEARSON LEHMAN BROTHERS TV COMMERCIAL.

Peak Season for Catalog Shopping

Lillian Vernon, a popular specialty catalog company, shipped out more than 4.3 million orders in fiscal 1991, or about 17,200 each working day. During its peak season, however, more than 35,000 orders were mailed to customers each day. On November 19, 1990, 54,000 orders went out the door—a record day for the company.

SOURCE: LILLIAN VERNON CORPORATION.

Longest Marriage

An eighty-sixth wedding anniversary was celebrated by Lazarus Rowe of Greenland, New Hampshire, and Molly Webber, both born in 1725, married in 1743, and died in 1829.

SOURCE: *GUINNESS BOOK OF WORLD RECORDS*, 1990.

Longest Engagement

The longest engagement on record was between Octavio Guillen, 82, and Adriana Martinez, 82, who were engaged for 67 years before they got married in June 1969, in Mexico City.

SOURCE: IBID.

Long Overdue

A German book was borrowed from a Cambridge University library by Colonel Robert Walpole in 1667 and found and returned in 1955, some 288 years later. SOURCE: IBID.

My Kind of an Opera

The shortest published opera was *Deliverance of Theseus* by Darius Milhaud; it was first performed in 1928 and lasted for 7 minutes, 27 seconds. SOURCE: IBID.

Best-Selling Book

An average of 2.2 million copies of the Bible are sold each year. SOURCE: AL NEUHARTH, "PLAIN TALK," *USA TODAY*, AUGUST 16, 1991.

Arriving on Time

From September 1987 to April 1989 the most on-time airlines were American West, Southwest, and American, arriving as scheduled 81 to 85 percent of the time.

SOURCE: DEPARTMENT OF TRANSPORTATION.

On-Time Flights

The following is a list of airlines and the percentage of their flights that arrived within 15 minutes of schedule during 1990:

Airline	Percentage
Pan Am	83.8%
America West	83.8%
Northwest	82.1%
Eastern	81.2%
U.S. Air	80.8%
Southwest	80.8%
Alaska	79.7%
American	79.0%
United	77.4%
TWA	77.1%
Delta	77.1%
Continental	76.9%

SOURCE: DEPARTMENT OF TRANSPORTATION.

Too Much Litigation, Too Many Lawyers

In 1989, approximately 18 million new civil cases were filed in U.S. state and federal courts. That's about 1 for every 10 adults. In the federal courts, the number of lawsuits filed each year has almost tripled in the past 30 years—from approximately 90,000 in 1960 to more than 250,000 in 1990. The annual cost for litigation to American society is an estimated $300 billion. An estimated 70 percent of the world's lawyers reside in America.

SOURCE: PRESIDENT'S COUNCIL ON COMPETITIVENESS.

Happy Birthday

Every day, 673,693 Americans have a birthday, and 3 million Americans will purchase birthday presents.

SOURCE: BUREAU OF THE CENSUS AND *AMERICAN DEMOGRAPHICS/ROPER*.

How Accurate Are the U.S. Census Takers?

It's estimated that the census—at 226,545,805 homes counted in 1980, was undercounted by 1.4 percent. In contrast, the 1990 census counted 245.8 million and a later updated figure was changed to 248 million in November 1990, a difference of about .9 percent.

SOURCE: CENSUS BUREAU.

A Longer School Year

A 1991 poll showed that, for the first time, a majority of Americans—51 percent—want the school year lengthened to 10 months, or 30 days more, from 180 days a year to 210 days.

SOURCE: GALLUP POLL FOR PHI DELTA KAPPA INTERNATIONAl.

Time Sharers Don't Always Share . . .

Former TV evangelist Jim Bakker convinced a lot of people to invest in his PTL theme park, but not all of these time sharers were able to get their share. 25,000 lifetime partners were able to use their privileges each year, whereas 95,000 were unable to get the annual vacation that was "due" them.

SOURCE: U.S. ATTORNEY GENERAL'S OFFICE.

Multicultural America

By the year 2000, one-third of the U.S. population will be nonwhite.

SOURCE: MARLENE A. CUMMINGS, "EDUCATION FOR A PLURALISTIC, DEMOCRATIC SOCIETY," *EDUCATION AND SOCIETY*, SUMMER 1988.

School Days, School Years . . .

The average SAT taker in 1991 had a total of 18.8 course years in high-school English, foreign language, mathematics, science, social sciences, and the arts, up from 18.1 years in 1987.

SOURCE: SCHOLASTIC APTITUDE TEST COLLEGE BOARD.

McWorld

There are 11,200 McDonald's restaurants in 52 countries worldwide, and a new McDonald's opens every 15 hours!

SOURCE: MCDONALD'S CORPORATION.

Number 75 Billion and Still Counting . . .

In 1989, McDonald's sold its 75-billionth hamburger.

SOURCE: IBID.

Going Under

In 1991, an estimated 1 million American consumers and businesses filed for bankruptcy. 92 percent of these were individuals.

SOURCE: AMERICAN BANKRUPTCY INSTITUTE.

Men Put on More Miles Than Women

American men drove an average of 16,632 miles in 1990 versus 9,543 for women drivers.

SOURCE: FEDERAL HIGHWAY ADMINISTRATION.

Preparing Your Own Return

In 1990, 53 percent of U.S. taxpayers prepared their own returns.

SOURCE: INTERNAL REVENUE SERVICE.

Let Block Do It!

The total U.S. tax returns filed in 1991 were 105.8 million; H & R Block prepared more than 15 million of them. The average charge by H & R Block for its tax preparation services was $51.25.

SOURCE: H & R BLOCK.

Busiest Grocery Shopping Days of the Week

Fridays appeal more to the over-55 crowd, whereas Saturdays draw the under-35 set.

SOURCE: *PROGRESSIVE GROCER*.

Early Detection of Baby Southpaws

A child's favored hand may become apparent as early as 8 months; by age 3, the preference is usually well-developed. Lefties sometimes mature more slowly than their right-handed peers, reaching puberty an average of 4 to 5 months later. They also tend to be about a half-inch shorter and 3 pounds lighter.

SOURCE: *GOOD HOUSEKEEPING*, FEBRUARY 1991.

Age of Mothers Influences Left-Handed Babies

10 to 15 percent of new mothers between 17 and 24 have left-handed babies, whereas mothers over 40 are more than twice as likely to have southpaws.

SOURCE: UNIVERSITY OF BRITISH COLUMBIA.

Bombarded with Ads

The average U.S. adult is bombarded with 3,000 marketing messages a day.

SOURCE: MARK LANDLER, KONRAD WALECIA, ZACHARY SHILLER, AND LOIS THERRIEN, "WHAT HAPPENED TO ADVERTISING?" *BUSINESS WEEK*, SEPTEMBER 23, 1991, P. 68.

Low Viewer Retention

Viewer retention of TV commercials has slipped dramatically in the past 4 years. In 1986, 64 percent of those surveyed could name a TV commercial they had seen in the previous 4 weeks. In 1990, just 48 percent could. SOURCE: VIDEO STORYBOARD TESTS.

Have Passport, Will Travel

The price of an adult passport rose from $42 to $65 on November 1, 1991.

Here are costs for previous years:

Year	Cost	Validity
1873	$3.00	2 years
1917	2.00	6 months
1920	10.00	2 years
1930	6.00	2 years
1932	10.00	2 years
1956	11.00	2 years
1959	11.00	3 years
1968	12.00	5 years
1974	13.00	5 years
1983	42.00	10 years
1991	65.00	10 years

NOTE: The cost includes fee plus execution costs.

SOURCE: DEPARTMENT OF STATE, BUREAU OF CONSULAR AFFAIRS.

Flights Abroad

The percentage of all flights from the United States to an international destination (excluding Canada and Mexico) is on the rise.

1977	1985	1990
8%	12%	18%

SOURCE: AIR TRANSPORT ASSOCIATION.

Trashing Times Square on New Year's Eve

An estimated 37 tons of trash were picked up in New York City's Times Square on New Year's Day 1991, as compared to 2 tons on an average day.

SOURCE: NEW YORK CITY DEPARTMENT OF SANITATION.

Twins Born in Different Years

On December 31, 1991, at precisely 11:56 P.M., Katherine Goddeke was born in Mount Clemens, Michigan. Her sister, Jessica, entered this world on January 1, 1992, at 12:14 A.M.

SOURCE: ASSOCIATED PRESS.

The Big Time Ball

The big ball that brings in the New Year when it drops over New York's Times Square weighs 200 pounds and has 180 light bulbs. The tradition began in 1907. SOURCE: ASSOCIATED PRESS.

Pasta Eating

Pasta consumption in the United States was 4.8 billion pounds in 1990. Annual per capita consumption is 19 pounds and is projected to reach 30 pounds per person by 2000. This amount compares to 60 pounds per person consumed by Italians each year. SOURCE: PETER D. FRANKLIN, "BORDEN USES ITS NOODLE TO BUILD LARGEST U.S. PASTA-MAKING PLANT," *COLUMBUS DISPATCH*, NOVEMBER 1, 1991.

Lawmakers Answering to Roll Call

In 1991, U.S. senators voted 97 percent of the time while House members averaged 95 percent. This is the highest level of voting participation since *Congressional Quarterly* began tracking recorded votes in 1953. In 1970, a low of 79 percent was recorded. William H. Natcher, D-Kentucky, has a 37-year unblemished record—he has not missed a vote during his career as a congressman, having voted 13,055 times since 1954.

SOURCE: *CONGRESSIONAL QUARTERLY.*

It's in the Mail . . . Overnight

The following are the four most active overnight/express services in the United States:

Carrier	Pieces delivered per day—1990
Federal Express	1,300,000
United Parcel Service	750,000
Airborne Express	400,000
U.S. Postal Service/Express Mail	200,000

SOURCES: EACH CARRIER.

Wilt the Stilt is High Scorer

Wilt Chamberlain claims to have slept with 20,000 women—an average of 1.4 a day for 40 years. SOURCE: WILT CHAMBERLAIN. *A VIEW FROM ABOVE.* VILLARD BOOKS, NEW YORK, 1991.

Per Capita Energy Consumption

With today's energy sources ranging from electricity to atomic power, the average American consumes about 327 million BTU per year. That's 96,000 kWh. Compare this amount to an unassisted human body that can do work equal to about 67 kWh per year. (Americans consume an average of 96,000 kWh in a year's time.) What this means is that each of us has an equivalent of 1,433 workers. That's a lot of servants—even for a king!

SOURCE: THOMAS R. KUHN, "ENERGY, EFFICIENCY, INGENUITY, THE HOPE FOR THE FUTURE," *VITAL SPEECHES*, AUGUST 15, 1991.

There's Nothing More to Invent . . .

In 10 A.D., the esteemed Roman engineer Julius Sextus Frontinus declared: "Inventions have long since reached their limit, and I see no hope for further developments."

During the John Quincy Adams administration (1825–1829), Congress came within 3 votes of terminating the U.S. Patent Office. The reason: there were representatives who believed that all the good ideas had already been patented and they wanted to save the taxpayers' money.

In 1899, the director of the U.S. Patent Office did it again. He advised President McKinley to close the office because "everything that can be invented has been invented."

SOURCE: AUTHORS' RESEARCH.

I'll See You on the Next Fifth Saturday in February

Once every 28 years, there are 5 Saturdays during the month of February.

SOURCE: AUTHORS' CALCULATIONS

Used Batteries

While some states have programs to recycle household batteries to reduce toxic waste, every year 2.7 billion batteries are junked.

SOURCE: EPA